Gender in Education

Multilingual Matters

Please contact us for the latest book information:
Multilingual Matters,
Bank House, 8a Hill Road,
Clevedon, Avon BS21 7HH,
England.

Gender in Education

Edited by
Eileen M. Byrne

MULTILINGUAL MATTERS LTD
Clevedon · Philadelphia

Library of Congress Cataloging-in-Publication Data

Gender in education / edited by Eileen M. Byrne
    p.   cm.
   Includes bibliographical references and index.
   1. Women—Education (Higher)   2. Women in education.
   3. Sex differences in education.   I. Byrne, Eileen M.
   LC1567.G46   1990
   370.19'345—dc20

British Library Cataloguing in Publication Data

   Gender in education
   1. Education. Sexism
   I. Title
   370.19345

ISBN 1-85359-106−8
ISBN 1-85359-105-X (pbk)

Multilingual Matters Ltd

Bank House, 8 Hill Road   &   1900 Frost Road, Suite 101
Clevedon, Avon BS21 7HH   Bristol, PA 19007
England.   USA.

This book is also available as a special issue of the journal
Evaluation and Research in Education (Vol. 3, No. 3, 1989).

Typeset by PhotoGraphics, Honiton.
Printed and bound in Great Britain by Short Run Press, Exeter.

PREFACE

In the decade and a half since the United Nations designated 1975 as International Women's Year to launch the Decade for Women, research into sex differences and gender in education has expanded, developed and deepened. It has been characterised by several trends. It has become more widespread, interdisciplinary and international, almost all major countries contributing to new research paradigms. It has, at last, become respectable, in direct measure to the extent that it is the more rigorous and scholarly—and better funded. And gender research has led the field in being increasingly *policy-oriented*.

Editorial selection therefore presents some difficulties. When the Decade began, accurate data on where women were (and weren't) in education and training were limited, and in some countries, non-existent. Sexism, sex-role stereotyping and discrimination were new concepts, and imperfectly defined both legislatively and for policy purposes. Accordingly, the first article sets the scene by reviewing the major contribution of the international organisations to improved gender-differentiation of data bases, as well as to developing new grounded theory.

Research has increasingly shown that sexist and sex-role stereotypic attitudes are already acquired and entrenched in the primary years—or younger. Scandinavia has led the field in school-based intervention research and accordingly, we asked Hildur Ve to report on new research on the first years of schooling in Norway.

Experts in the field will know that much of the pioneer research on gender came out of America, followed closely by Western European initatives. But the 1980s have seen a questioning of the validity of transferring research findings *mutatis mutandis* across countries and across cultures. Shirley Sampson's overview of a decade of Australian research suggests that Australian findings by no means always replicate the received wisdom of Western European research. Each country needs to sustain its own research as well as take account of internationally valid findings.

Evidence persists that despite some progress in reducing sexism in schooling, women still do not reach the apex of hierarchies, power, higher education or economically important science and technology in equal proportions. Cascading losses still occur as girls move up systems. And without more women at the top, changes are not likely to occur below. This issue therefore also looks at women at the tertiary level. Margaret Sutherland, using qualitative and diagnostic methodology, reports on some of her recent research on women professors in Universities, with important messages for policymakers implicit in her findings. From Berlin comes a report of research which, equally qualitative and diagnostic, investigates the 'profile of success' or otherwise of that *rara avis* of nontraditional women, the woman engineering student. And from Australia, the interim findings of the UQ WISTA project suggest that institutions have no alibi for inaction in accounting for women's underrecruitment to specific scientific disciplines in their own institutions: an institutional ecology approach.

1

The Decade has produced an unprecedented range of scholarly and seminal books and published research reports on gender. We have selected three books to review to represent different research approaches. Carol Gilligan's *In a Different Voice* is a seminal and widely relevant work which challenges current received wisdom using essentially qualitative research methods and represents a contribution to new theory. It is centrally relevant to educators in the context of our need to reconstruct how we handle moral education and human relationships education in schooling. *Analyzing Gender*, by contrast, is a recent example of the wide-ranging interdisciplinary research reviews which have increasingly provided the *broader* reconstructions of gender against which educators need to set their specifically focused gender research projects. And as a new report of such a focused study, we chose to review the widely-publicised *A Gender Agenda*, both to interest those who believe that intervention in the primary years is critical and as an example of new empirical traditional research. It also, however, serves to illustrate the weaknesses of over-reliance on empirical research methodology where this is not grounded in rigorous critical theory.

We began the Decade by focusing on girls and women. Research in the last fifteen years establishes, however, beyond reasonable doubt that the main problem about girls and women is usually boys and men—that is *gender relations* and not issues of only one sex without the other. Research in the 1990s now needs to focus on eliminating *gender bias*—but not on eliminating gender.

Eileen M. Byrne

GROUNDED THEORY AND THE SNARK SYNDROME: THE ROLE OF THE INTERNATIONAL ORGANISATIONS IN RESEARCH IN GENDER IN EDUCATION

Eileen M. Byrne

Department of Education, University of Queensland, St. Lucia, QLD 4067, Australia

Abstract Research into sex differences, sex-role stereotyping and gender issues in education has expanded rapidly with increased funding and greater respectability since International Women's Year, 1975. Concurrently, we have seen a gradual move from quantitative to more qualitative research. This has both helped, and been helped by, the increased role of the international organisations, whose role in ensuring or providing improved data bases, and in helping to develop new grounded theory, is reviewed here.

In recent years, an increasingly sharp debate has developed about the merits and demerits of quantitative and qualitative research and their allegedly value-free or value-laden status. One issue central to this debate is the perceivedly more limited nature of generalisations which can be established by qualitative work in the social sciences. Another problem is how to ensure that research findings are what Sowden & Keeves (1988) describe as 'replicable and robust' and convincing to other researchers. Miles & Huberman (1984) identify twelve tactics for confirming findings in qualitative research, which include a rational process for *weighting the evidence*; the need for more rigorous *searching for spurious relationships* in a way which distinguishes cause-and-effect relationships from mere co-existence of factors; and *looking for negative evidence* which serves, *inter alia*, to test existing received wisdom.

The writer has identified a further process which was common at the onset of the Decade and which has not yet been quite eliminated despite improved data bases and increasingly scholarly approaches to gender research in education. This has been identified in recent research (Byrne, 1989) as *the Snark syndrome*. In Lewis Carroll's *The Hunting of the Snark*, the poem opens

Just the place for a Snark, the Bellman cried . . .
Just the place for a Snark! I have said it twice:
That alone should encourage the crew.
Just the place for a Snark! I have said it thrice:
What I tell you three times is true.

Rigorous reexamination of much received wisdom about sex differences (nature or nurture?); about where women are or aren't in schooling and post-schooling;

about single sex and coeducation; about same-sex role modelling; and about the advances and setbacks of girls in schooling and women in education, have proved it increasingly to have little more basis in hard data or logical critical theory than having been oft repeated. Hypotheses repeated three (or thirty) times without regular recourse to data analyses, have acquired a spurious but enduring 'truth', on the basis that what is told us three times is true.

For this reason, the work of Glaser & Strauss on the development of grounded theory has been important in the last decade or so. Glaser & Strauss (1972) define *substantive theory* as 'the formulation of concepts and their interrelation into a set of hypotheses for a given substantive area—such as . . . education—based on research in the area' (p. 288). They see it as deriving from qualitative research, and as the basis on which *grounded formal theory* is generated.

Athough they discuss the production of substantive theory from qualitative research primarily in the context of fieldwork, they nevertheless see substantive theory as the end product, by no means always needing major empirical studies to justify retaining multiple and related hypotheses *grounded in data*. Substantive theory is, they argue, first formulated in order to see which of diverse formal theories are applicable to a problem or an area, and plays a central role in revising formal theory. They see substantive theory as a strategic link in the formulation and development of formal theory based on data. '*We have called the latter 'grounded' formal theory to contrast it with formal theory based on logical speculation.*' (p. 300)

It is in this context of grounded theory, that this article reviews the contribution of the major international organisations to research on gender in education over the last fifteen years. The differentiation of formal theory based on logical speculation from formal theory *grounded in data* is seen as central to the development of new understanding of gender issues in education.

It could be argued that the real starting point for major international review of educational policy and the education of women was the seminal report to the United Nations on the status of women in Sweden from the Royal Swedish Ministry for Foreign Affairs (1968). This arose from Resolution No. 1133(XLI) of the UN's Economic and Social Council aimed at raising the status of women. The Swedish report made it clear that special measures for women were useless unless countries also agreed 'to abolish the conditions which tend to assign certain privileges, obligations or rights to men'. In particular, the Swedish Government reported that 'the difficulties confronting adult women on the labour market today are largely attributable to their inferior education compared with that of men. They were not given the *same* chances in their youth' (Royal Swedish Ministry for Foreign Affairs, 1968: 25). Education policy, declared Sweden to the United Nations, must be based on the principle that '*equal means the same*': equal did not, the report declared, mean 'equivalent but different'.

In the previous year, 1967, UNESCO had embarked on a long-term programme to promote equality of educational opportunity between the sexes. Issues to be explored by commissioned research included coeducation, equal access for girls and women to the three levels of education, equal access to the *same* education, and equal access to technical and vocational education as part of the education process.

By the early 1970s, it had become clear that there was no general agreement on which problems facing girls and women were *generic*, that is cross-cultural and cross-national, and which problems were *idiosyncratic* to particular education systems or cultures. Moreover, no clear agreement existed on where girls and women actually were (and weren't) in different sectors of education and training. This was partly because many countries did not possess data banks which were sex-divided at each level and in each stream of their systems. Yet the received wisdom circulating in the early 1970s in the higher levels of administration, was that sex differentiation in basic access was an anachronism in developed countries. Through the Snark syndrome of constant repetition, we were told that girls and women had now caught up. Hence the first issue reviewed here, is that of basic access.

The Access Question

Education administrators have long argued that schooling did not discriminate against girls and that the schooling system as such was open to all with the relevant age, ability and aptitude. Differentiation of participation rates, curricular options and retention was, they argued, a result of girls' own aspirations and 'choices': the blaming-the-victim or deficit theory approach. This, indeed, has been the overtly argued rationale behind the entrenched public opposition of Ministries of Education in many Western countries to the inclusion of education in sex discrimination legislation. Dominant theory argued as late as the early 1970s that there were no legal or structural barriers to equal access; and that if girls and women did not 'choose' to study at the same levels, or the same curricula, or the same vocational training as boys and men, this was either because of generic and innately programmed sex differences, or because of 'natural' differences in interest and aspiration. That is, the Snark syndrome was operating in the constant repetition of these assertions without any serious statistical or research-based evidence to support them. A range of research reviews by international organis-ations, however, have now established beyond doubt that

(i)   there have been (and arguably still are) structural and systemic barriers to girls' equal access to the *same* education and training in many countries and cultures, and

(ii) the cause of girls' different patterns of participation cannot be generic to girls and women and must be idiosyncratic to systems and cultures, because of the high degree of variability of levels and 'choices' of female partici-pation in courses in different countries and systems.

We look first at technical and vocational, and secondly at basic education in this context.

Technical and vocational education for girls

Perhaps the sharpest distinctions have emerged in technical and vocational education. UNESCO's (1968) comparative study of the access of girls and women to technical and vocational education across 87 countries, asked whether Consti-tutions, Acts or Regulations made distinctions in access between girls and boys to this sector; and all countries replied in the negative. Yet this detailed study simultaneously recorded special programmes of technical education 'for women' or 'for men', from Italy to Iran, from Ecuador to the Netherlands. The consider-able actual data in this report regularly contradicted the motherhood statements of policy intent issued by different countries. Thus Burma, describing its scholarship scheme as 'without discrimination as to sex', recorded 210 vocational scholarships for girls, but 1062 for boys—852 agricultural training scholarships being designated for males only. Across the study as a whole, UNESCO found that:

- technical education for girls was less accessible than for boys, more limited in range and scope and followed the sextyping of the labour market;
- the phenomenon of 'cascading losses' occurred: that is, female proportions were less at each stage of progression from semi-skilled to skilled to technician level.

In 1974, UNESCO published a Revised Recommendation concerning Technical and Vocational Education, adopted by the General Conference in Paris on 19th November 1974, which laid down among other principles, that technical and vocational education must be available equally to women as to men, that women should have the *same* educational opportunities as men for preparing for work outside the home, that special provision should be made for women returning to the labour force after family responsibilities, and that vocational guidance should cover the same range of training and employment for girls and women as for boys and men.

An EEC study of equality of education for girls in nine countries (Byrne, 1978), however, found that the vocational and technical education systems still showed the two 1968 trends, but in addition, highlighted other structural and systemic factors needing review. Technical education was not only sex-differentiated to match a sex-segregated labour market, but had structural barriers barring cross-sex enrolments. Female-dominated training generally led to lower level qualifications and had a more limited transfer value. Some countries separated out technical education for girls and boys as early as 13–14 years of age. This might be either in separate schools like Italy's *istituti industriali* and *istituti femminile* or in separate streams in secondary or technical schools as in the Netherlands at that time. And female participation rates in technical and vocational education were almost universally lower, still. Countries with strong separation of technical from academic education in the earlier *school years* were also those with the strongest sex-differentiation in participation.

But by 1980, it was clear that very little progress had been made on any of UNESCO's 1974 recommendations, and that in some respects, women's position was relatively worsening. Reports prepared for a UNESCO Category IV Congress in 1980 (Byrne, 1980a) on technical and vocational education of women, confirmed a range of trends which still represented static growth in relation to general world economic and educational expansion, in many developing countries. Firstly, basic illiteracy had, if anything, increased over the decade. Secondly, vocational enrolments for girls in African countries, in South Asia and in the Pacific remained well behind male enrolments. In those countries where female enrolments seemed high, further examination of Ministry curricula and schemes showed that 'technical' education for girls was either wholly domestic science and family education (Indonesia) or leading almost wholly to 'feminine' low-paid work. Iraq's skilled female workers proved to be mainly dressmakers. In Bangladesh, the four work experience areas in schooling were agriculture, industry, social welfare and home economics: but the first two were restricted to males, the latter two to females. In the Philippines, girls were given training in handicrafts, cooking and sewing while boys were in workshops or gardens. Almost all Malaysian home science, welfare and steward students were female. In Thailand, a vocational survey of the Manpower Planning Office revealed that school leavers from Home Economics Schools have consistently much higher unemployment rates than those for agricultural or commercial schools (78% as compared with 55% and 45%), a finding that is replicated in Western countries (Luxembourg, Italy). In those countries with significant female enrolments (Thailand, Burma, Sri Lanka) girls were still centred in 'feminine' areas of technical and vocational education (Byrne, 1980a), mostly commercial or home economics programmes (UNESCO, 1979: 75).

Dupont's (1981) later study of sex differentiation in curricula confirmed the continuing existence of sex-segregation of vocational and technical education: *'although boys and girls follow broadly the same curricula, the differences creep in as soon as vocational experience, guidance or training are involved . . . the omnipresence of domestic science as an optional subject tends to accustom girls to the role of mother-wife-housewife without broadening their options'* (p. 45). In all of the seven countries surveyed by Dupont, the channelling of girls towards special 'feminine' courses *'clearly does not at present constitute a means of promoting the participation of women in economic, social and cultural development'* (p. 43). Further limitations confirmed by Dupont were the narrower range of options offered to girls and the sex-segregation of the teachers in a differentiated vocational system, thus both depriving both sexes of pupils of alternative role models and limiting the opportunities for women teachers. Jordan had, for example, no industrial or agricultural courses for girls and hence Jordanian women could not be trained to teach for these occupational areas; a self-perpetuating problem. A later international review by the OECD reported the same trends as those outlined in this section, across a range of developed countries (OECD, 1986).

The third main finding of the 1980 UNESCO review (Byrne, 1980a) was of automatic male priority in *educational planning*. In a number of African and Asian countries, where World Bank or IDA develoment projects were approved, governments often planned overtly for male priority. Sierra Leone, for example, had a deficiency of secondary places in the ratio of less than half girls to boys in the early 1970s. The IDA approved development plan of grant aid provided eleven new secondary schools for 2400 boys but *no provision for technical education for girls*. The planned ten-year programme remained at 2149 girls and 5726 boys— an indefensible endorsement of discriminatory planning. Such girls' schools as existed in the 1970s in Sierra Leone were also centred in only one province, with no plans for extensions to female school hostel accommodation, or expansion in rural areas to extend girls' access.

In 1980, these international studies were therefore providing decisive evidence to contradict the received wisdom that there was parity of basic access for girls to technical education.

Basic schooling

The dissonance between 'official' theory and theory *grounded in data* also emerges even more sharply in relation to access to *basic schooling*, recently thoroughly documented by two further UNESCO studies. In a study published in 1980 on male and female enrolment and illiteracy (Slama & Sauvageot, 1980), two UNESCO consultants analysed dropout and wastage and rates of literacy across different regions and countries of the world. The study highlighted a serious *aggregation of inequality*. For example, in Africa over 60% of illiterates were women, but additionally of the 40% of girls enrolled in schools, a significant proportion dropped out much earlier than boys, and the ratio of girls to boys also decreased consistently from one level to another. The sex disparity is actually increasing in Africa and South Asia, particularly in the 6–11 age group, which has disturbing implications for women's future in those regions. Overall, in 1985 in the world as a whole there were about 37,000,000 more boys than girls enrolled in the 6–11 age group, 34,780,000 of these in developing countries. The disparity will continue to grow unless there is a strong political commitment to change (Slama & Sauvageot, 1980: 16–17). At secondary level, female enrolments in India, Indonesia and many Pacific countries are *falling relatively*. This study highlighted the need for improved sociological and cultural studies to analyse the reasons (apart from excessive population growth) and to design contextually relevant counter-programmes.

A parallel UNESCO study on the school education of girls (Deblé, 1980) looked at dropout and wastage over the decade 1967–1977. The findings rightly differentiated between groups of countries in relation to attitude on the one hand (Latin America has more girls in schooling proportionately than Africa and less overt male prejudice according to some studies) and culture base on the other. Recurring throughout the study were three main findings:

– fewer girls still consistently had access to schooling at all in the first place;
– more girls lost ground as pupils moved up in grades, in over half of the countries surveyed: cascading losses again;
– female dropout rates tended to be higher.

In twenty-four African countries, active discrimination in favour of boys was recorded as resulting in very considerable sex differences. In fifteen Asian countries, more boys completed primary education and therefore more entered secondary education. And when girls moved on to vocational education, they had to move into sex-segregated streams, the 'feminine' of which was heavily biased towards the domestic role. Deblé suggests that

> the multifarious causes of female wastage are approached by intuition rather than precise research—(we note) the strong tendency in the most disadvantaged countries to say that there is nothing to be done, that all other things being equal, boys will always get on better than girls. (Deblé, 1980: 122)

Her conclusions included a need for more girls' schools, boarding hostels and teacher training programmes for girls, including facilities for the transport and accommodation of primary school teachers in rural areas, and that '*without a fundamental and resolute will to bring about change, finding expression in carefully studied and coordinated practical measures, equal access to education for girls and boys might well prove unattainable in several parts of the world*' (p. 30).

Curricular Differences: Interest or Structural?

A second area in which the Snark syndrome still operates is the constantly re-asserted claim that the sex-differentiation of curricular choices is a matter of 'natural interest', and that boys and girls choose subjects which accord with a biologically predetermined mutually exclusive 'male' or 'female' temperament and *persona*. This is still reasserted by Ministries, school principals, curriculum development officers, despite many country-based individual academic research studies which authenticate alternative theories. It has been used as an alibi for inaction by education administrators on this issue.

The role of the international organisations has been of particular influence here. They have, over the last two decades

- raised the gender debate to a serious politically and professionally accredited level;
- sponsored research cross-nationally and cross-culturally to improve diagnosis and understanding of causes of sex-differentiation;
- improved international cooperation and exchange of expertise between experts;
- produced credible and monitored improved data bases, not only in statistics but also in records of country-by-country educational practices and experiences.

Among these, the Nordic Council (an international Scandinavian advisory body to the Nordic Council of Ministers) has developed, over the last two decades, a major professional debate disseminated by regular publications, based on research and expertise from Denmark, Iceland, Finland, Norway and Sweden. The data, professional expertise and research culled by the work of the Nordic Council, has established beyond reasonable doubt that, *inter alia*, sex-differentiation of curricular choices arises from such factors as sex-stereotyping in classrooms, sex-stereotypic attitudes of teachers, sexism and sex-stereotyping in educational books and materials, lack of teaching on stereotyping or non-sexist child development theory in teacher training. That is, the evidence from the Nordic Council totally rejects the hypothesis that 'natural interest' unaffected by educational environment causes sex-differentiation of curricular choice (Nordic Council, 1979).

The *grounded hypothesis* that sex-differentiation in curriculum arises from *constructed sex roles* influenced by national culture and teacher/parent/community attitudes, is supported also by a seven-country study commissioned by UNESCO in 1978–80 as part of the Plan of Action of the World Conference of International Women's Year (1975). The study (Dupont, 1981) is a thorough analysis of curricula, systems, course-tracking and research evidence from a variety of countries. Many of the official bodies in those countries adduced alleged reasons of female inferiority (psychologically or physically or in religious terms) as the reason for either excluding girls from some curricula or limiting women's progress in technical training.

But the evidence from the same countries simultaneously confirmed girls' equal capacity, since many of them (Portugal, Madagascar, Jamaica) also provided evidence of education change and of some increasing female enrolments in non-traditional areas. Dupont's conclusions confirmed the influence of a range of structural and cultural factors which frequently denied girls *the same curricula* as boys. Equal did not mean the same: at best, in theory it meant 'equivalent'. Structurally, homecraft and sewing were universally compulsory for girls and manual and industrial (technical) subjects for boys—by regulation, by curriculum structure, by timetabling, by cultural pressure. Almost universally, single-sex girls' schools did not offer the same curriculum as boys (including, sometimes, in maths or science), or taught a different curriculum under the same label. Teachers' attitudes, stereotyping in textbooks and school guidance were widely evident as influencing curricular 'choice' where this was theoretically possible.

A later review commissioned by the OECD (1986) discourages a view that this is now history and that educational reforms are removing either sex-differentiation or gender inequality. The regular monitoring of improved statistics cross-nationally enables us to recognise that despite *'the very marked and near-universal growth of female enrolments in the main educational branches and sectors (there is) the rigid division by gender that is still apparent in terms of school subjects and the tracks pursued post-school'* (OECD, 1986: 10).

The OECD report still records that 'some assert that formal educational opportunities are now equal between the sexes and that recent years have witnessed the realisation of actual equality in terms of courses studied and qualifications obtained', which given the mass of published research since 1975, is the Snark syndrome at its acutest. The OECD defends the role of cross-national statistical stocktaking: 'Time and again, the demonstration of clear injustices with simple facts has proved sufficient to set in motion educational reforms' (OECD, 1986).

As more detailed international and cross-national reviews are published, we are able to move behind generalisations to use data analyses to focus more precisely on causes and effects. The OECD (1986) review confirms both continuing negative patterns and improving trends; but the more sophisticated data available enables us to see modifications and qualifications to these. While women had, for example, increased their proportion of higher education enrolments in the 1980s, this was *not* in nontraditional areas, and 'precisely those courses or programmes in which women are concentrated are those singled out as at risk of suffering downgrading in terms of academic standing and resources' (p. 27).

By the early 1980s, girls had narrowed or eliminated the retention rate gap and the qualifications gap in academic secondary education in most developed countries—but not in technical or vocational courses. And the continued marked sex-differentiation in curricular options has resulted also in female 'tracks' or 'lines' in secondary education which have a declining value in the job market. Moreover, 'the fact that the most valued courses and qualifications (in higher education) as they change over time, remain male domains means that the increased female participation in them may well be only enough to ensure that the position of young women has not actually deteriorated' (OECD, 1986: 24).

A similar data-analysis by UNESCO (1987) of women in higher education gives rise to the same qualified judgement. Women were approaching half of all higher education students in many developed countries (except Greece, 40% and Japan 23%). They were, however, only between 18% and 24% of women students in the natural sciences in any world region; and women academic staff in the natural sciences ranged from 4.6% (Canada) and 9.9% (Norway) to 38% (Portugal) in the mid 1980s.

And this and UNESCO data, enable us to refute another Snark syndrome theory: that of same-sex role modelling.

Same-Sex-Role Modelling and Enrolments

It has been widely asserted by academic researchers, by administrators and by heads of educational institutions, that the real problem about increasing female enrolments, and particularly in non-traditional areas, is the lack of female role models. 'If only we had more women staff, we'd have more women students'. This is also an acute attack of the Snark syndrome and proves to have, on examination, no empirical basis whatever for supporting the hypotheses. (It is, one should add, also a classic use of deficit theory (blaming women) to avoid the need to look for alternative causes and strategies.) But it does not stand up to examination.

In the UNESCO dropout and wastage study, Deblé found that 'The most recent UNESCO data on the proportion of women in the teaching profession and the proportion of girls at school *show, whatever the level of education, no statistical relation*' (Deblé, 1980: 104).

This and other contemporary evidence led this writer to analyse further the statistical tables and analyses in UNESCO yearbooks, OECD reports and EEC data from EUROSTAT where available, over the decade 1975–1985. In no country, sector or subsector could even a first-level statistical correlation be found. As a result, we built in a further check on the hypothesis in a new Australia-wide research project. In a complex and detailed study of women in science and technology in Australia, a data analysis of women students at undergraduate, masters and PhD levels and women academic staff, in twenty scientific and technological disciplines across ten institutions, showed no correlation at any level of a consistency to support the hypothesis. The evidence from the UQ WISTA study refutes entirely any hypothesis that relative proportions of women staff and women students are in any way correlated. Same-sex-role modelling may break-the-male-stereotype; but it does not, of itself, increase female enrolments (Byrne, 1989a: Chapter IV; Byrne, 1989b).

One can echo Deblé's findings of ' *the inadequacy of statistical information—lack of data, lack of relevant processing or lack of dissemination—as to how girls accede to education and then pursue their schooling . . . Ignorance of the facts greatly handicaps the search for effective solutions. Too many assertions are founded on impressions*' (Deblé, 1980: 126–7).

Role Modelling and Sexism in Educational Materials

This is not to say that same-sex-role modelling does not take place or is irrelevant to the issue. It does, in fact, act to break-the-male-stereotype in the context of the media; of images in books and in male:female representation in educational materials and games; and in other transmitted image contexts. Twenty years (even ten) ago, the hypothesis that sexism and sex-role stereotyping in books and materials was influential in affecting girls' and boys' educational experiences, decisions, choices, was regarded as a gleam in an avant-garde feminist eye. The international organisations have increasingly culled the research and expert opinion of specialists in many countries on qualitative causes of sex differentiation, and their cross-national and cross-cultural data and evidence establish beyond doubt that this is a major, credible, central policy issue still needing strategic and decisive counter-strategies in the 1990s.

The special data report prepared for the Standing Conference of (22) European Ministers of Education in 1979 (Kohnstamm Institute, 1979) confirmed 'sex-role stereotyping to an extreme degree' in the curricular materials of a range of countries; but at that period only the Scandinavian countries were recorded as having strategies for changing traditional patterns. UNESCO commissioned a series of studies of the portrayal of women and men in textbooks and educational materials in the 1980s in four regions (Asia and Pacific, the Arab World; Northern

America and Western Europe) and in Norway, France, Zambia, China and the Ukraine. The detailed and widely-ranging evidence from many cultures and countries confirmed a number of now well-known facts: women's relative invisibility; the image of girls and women as domestic infrastructure, as more passive, as less adventurous, as less capable, as more dependent; the lack of women portrayed in roles now normal in the relevant society (driving a car, managing a business, working with machines)—all of these were found in all recorded countries. However, the UNESCO synthesis report (Michel, 1986) does report some encouraging new non-sexist materials and programmes to remediate the widespread finding that the images and examples in books were not only very sextyped but *very out-of-date to the point of anachronism*, in relation to women's actual roles in each society.

Single-Sex or Coeducation?

Another issue in which the Snark syndrome plays a prominent role, is the policy controversy over single-sex versus coeducational schooling. The oversimplistic hypothesis expounded by West European (mainly English) feminists that single-sex schooling advantages girls, has little basis in scholarly analysis. It has also been unselectively propounded in that theorists have:

(a) not always identified what the precise advantage was (retention? progression? higher qualifications?), nor what evidence there was of a cause-and-effect relationship, or

(b) not identified or weighed in balance, correlational disadvantages (restricted curricula; lack of experience of competing with boys).

In particular, where the alleged advantage was rather vaguely described as improved female self-esteem, there has been no serious attempt to authenticate this as a cause-and-effect dyadic relationship, by controlling for other concurrent social or educational factors.

The bank of cross-national and cross-cultural international reports over the Decade becomes one source of data and evidence which has been, therefore, useful and credible in testing the hypothesis by examining its grounding or otherwise in even first-level data.

If we review the range of data and evidence presented over the last two decades, two main findings emerge: the statistics do not support the hypothesis; and the actual disadvantages of single-sex schooling are measurable and more substantial. Firstly, if single-sex schooling as such advantaged girls in retention or progression, we would expect to find consistently higher overall female retention and progression rates in those countries with major single-sex provision—both in developed countries (for example Ireland, Italy) or developing countries (for example, Jordan, Afghanistan)—and we do not.

Secondly, if single-sex schooling advantaged girls in encouraging them to take more nontraditional subjects, courses or tracks, we would expect those countries with significant single-sex provision to have higher female nontraditional enrolments. We do not find this, except where other factors of heavier weight also occur. Thus Egypt had higher nontraditional female enrolments in technical education than all other Arab States (Byrne, 1980). All of these had single-sex education, but only Egypt under Sadat had combined this with a conscious policy of building more residental hostels at girls' technical schools to encourage non-metropolitan enrolments in sectors of rational economic interest, but simultaneously to meet with the cultural and religious restrictions of the indigenous society. The higher female enrolments coexisted with single-sex learning: they were not caused by it. Other analyses of cross-national and cross-cultural data provide no ground whatever in statistics for supporting the much-repeated hypothesis of single-sex advantage.

When we look at qualitative evidence from international studies and country reports, evidence cited in the first section in relation to technical and vocational education becomes also relevant. In none of the UNESCO surveys published over the last two decades, can we find any substantial evidence that where courses, tracks or schools are sex-segregated, they offer the *same* curricula to girls as to boys. Dupont's (1981) study also showed a totally consistent pattern of a separate girls' curriculum which lacked either the technical crafts, or advanced maths, or lacked equal science provision, or the same agricultural curriculum. And the sex-differentiation was sharper in single-sex schools. Self-esteem alone will not provide girls with access to subjects and qualifications they are not offered.

West European researchers will, of course, argue that the issue is rather one of male-dominated discourse in mixed schools, and of male territoriality in mixed learning. This is recognised, and is dealt with (and refuted) by the writer in other publications. The issue here is that access to the extensive quantitative and qualitative data and evidence across a range of countries enables us to move from the overgeneralised unqualified and unfounded hypothesis that 'single-sex education is better for girls' to a series of more accurately grounded hypotheses. For example:

- single-sex vocational and technical education acts as a critical filter for girls and women;
- single-sex education limits curricular subjects offered to girls: many of these are critical to their vocational advancement;
- single-sex education as such does not result in significant increases in female enrolments, female progression or female participation in nontraditional areas.

Improved Data and Research Bases and Educational Policy

Each international report published by the EEC, UNESCO, Nordic Council, OECD, is based in turn on data and policy reports produced by member countries. The data is, therefore, only as sound as its source. One of the contributions of the international organisations over the last two decades has been to use Statistical Offices like the professionally-staffed Eurostat in Luxembourg and UNESCO's extensive consultancy services, to help countries to standardise the collection of sex-differentiated statistics and to harmonise the interpretation of these across systems. Academic analysis of both published cross-national data and research based on widely varying country reports, has enabled us to support grounded hypotheses of increasingly targetted specificity, as a basis for future policy change and reform. This matches an increased thrust towards *international* definition of research priorities, research objectives and hypotheses as a basis for policy on the part of all international organisations, in the area of gender in education. Each initiative has focused on girls and women, partly because of their universal greater disadvantage and partly because of the focus of the 1975–1985 Decade for Women. But increasingly, research has highlighted ricochet disadvantages for males also in excessive sex-differentiation in education.

In 1975, the World Conference of International Women's Year in Mexico City, published a *World Plan of Action* for achieivng international and national objectives, which included

- equal access at every level of education;
- extending 'coeducational technical and vocational training in basic skills' to women as well as men in industry and agriculture;
- increased literacy and civic education of women, especially in rural regions;
- reducing wastage and dropout from schooling and education by girls and women.

It is clear that many of the studies cited derive from this overall policy thrust. In 1976, the Council of Ministers of Education of the European Community passed a Resolution (9.2.1976) which declared that the achievement of equal opportunity in all forms of education was an essential aim of all member States, and that its importance should be seen in relation to all economic and social policy. A later Resolution (13.12.1976) adopted an action programme which included a Community initiative to initiate '*the design and development of specific actions to ensure equal educational opportunities for girls*'. The first study arising from this (Byrne, 1978) served as a diagnostic analysis based on a nine country survey of statistics and evidence of education systems and participation. Since then, the use by the EEC of regular research policy studies to underpin new policy initiatives in vocational training, non-sexist education and equality in youth provision, has become standard.

UNESCO published its first Medium-Term Plan, approved by General Conference at its XIXth Conference in Nairobi for the period 1977–1982, as a step towards focusing on defined world and regional objectives, and which included major sections on gender equality in education and training. This, and its second Medium-Term Plan for 1984–89 approved in Paris at an extraordinary General Conference in 1982, have proved the spur to considerably increased investment in research and enquiry in gender issues. This has enabled us to improve to some extent our research approaches in the context of the issues raised in the opening paragraphs of this article: how far findings are 'replicable and robust', how evidence should be weighted, which relationships prove to be spurious, and where there is negative evidence.

But we are far from arrived at a scholarly and thorough understanding of gender issues. The UNESCO Second Medium-Term Plan recognises the decisive role that education plays in 'making women aware of their own aspirations, their real potential and their rights' (para 14023). But the Plan also recorded in 1983 that, despite a decade of work:

There is no coherent body of theoretical knowledge on the subject, be it the scientific knowledge needed to put paid to a great many received ideas about the differences between the sexes, or elementary statistical information, for instance, of the kind that would give an accurate picture of women's real activity in the national economy. A great deal of ignorance and prejudice and many mistaken ideas still persist concerning women . . . (UNESCO, 1983: para 14022).

There is need, *inter alia*, for more research to be targeted on the interface of the sex-differentiation of education and training practices and women's worsening position in the labour force; and on continuing sex bias in teaching and learning practices. Until then, the Snark syndrome is still alive and well in bureaucracies, educational administration and government. Our continued task in the 1990s is to counter this with improved conceptualisation as well as improved data.

References

Byrne, Eileen M. (1978) *Equality of Education and Training for Girls*. Commission of the European Communities Studies, Education Series 9, Brussels.

—— (1980a) *Technical & Vocational Education for Women—The Way Ahead*. UNESCO, ED/80/CONF/401, Paris, June 1980.

—— (1980b) *Women's Work, Men's Work—New Perspectives for Change*. UNESCO, ED/80/CONF.708/3, Paris, 14 August 1980.

—— (1989a) *Women in Science and Technology: The Institutional Ecology Approach*. Interim Research Report (UQ WISTA), Department of Education, University of Queensland.

—— (1989b) *Role Modelling and Mentorship as Policy Mechanisms: The Need for New Directions*. Department of Education, University of Queensland.

Deblé, Isabelle (1980) *The School Education of Girls*. Paris: UNESCO.

Dupont, Beatrice (1981) *Unequal Education: Sex Differences in Secondary School Curricula*. Paris: UNESCO.

Glaser, B.G. and Strauss, A.L. (1972) Discovery of substantive theory: A basic strategy underlying qualitative research. In W. Filstead (ed.) *Qualitative Methodology: Firsthand Involvement with the Social World* (pp. 288–304). Chicago: Markham Publishing Co.

Kohnstamm Institute (1979) Education and equality of opportunity for girls and women. Data report, Standing Conference of European Ministers of Education, 10–13 June 1979, CME/XI/79/5.

Michel Andrée (1986) *Down with Stereotypes: Eliminating Sexism from Children's Literature and Books*. Paris: UNESCO. (The Michel report is based on detailed country reports from Norway, France, Zambia, China, the Arab World, Ukraine, Asia and Pacific, and North America and Western Europe, all published by UNESCO.)

Miles, M.B. and Huberman, A.M. (1984) *Qualitative Data Analysis: A Sourcebook of New Methods*. Beverley Hills CA: Sage.

Nordic Council of Ministers (1979) Sex roles and education. Report to the 11th Session of the Standing Conference of European Ministers of Education, CME/XI(79)6.

OECD (1986) *Girls & Women in Education*. Paris: OECD.

Royal Swedish Ministry of Foreign Affairs (1968) The status of women in Sweden. Report to United Nations, Stockholm.

Slama, S. and Sauvageot, C. (1980) *Comparative Analysis of Male and Female Enrolment and Illiteracy*. Paris: UNESCO.

Sowden, S. and Keeves, J.P. (1988) Analysis of evidence in humanistic studies. In J.P. Keeves (ed.) *Educational Research, Methodology and Measurement: An International Handbook* (p. 524). Oxford: Pergamon Press.

UNESCO (1968) *Comparative Study on Access of Girls and Women to Technical and Vocational Education*. ED/MD/3, Paris, 20 December 1968.

—— (1979) *Developments in Technical and Vocational Education: A Comparative Study*. Paris: UNESCO.

—— (1983) *Second Medium Term Plan 1984–1989*. Paris: UNESCO (4XC/4).

—— (1987) *Survey on the Representation of Women in Higher Education and Research*. Paris: UNESCO.

EQUALITY BETWEEN GIRLS AND BOYS IN THE PRIMARY YEARS: A NORWEGIAN ACTION RESEARCH PROJECT

Hildur Ve

Institute of Sociology, University of Bergen, N5000 Bergen, Norway

Abstract An interdisciplinary action research project in Norway has recently been conducted to attempt to produce a gender-neutral learning environment in the first weeks and years of primary schooling. Among the interim findings discussed here, the greater reluctance of boys to move away from already established male-stereotypic behaviour, than girls from female-stereotypic behaviour, is significant even in the first weeks of schooling.

There is widespread agreement that sex-role stereotyping about male and female roles in work and family, begins in the primary years. Perceptions as to 'normal' or 'suitable' (and mutually exclusive) roles for boys and girls, men and women, have been reinforced by teachers, by the learning environment and by peer group pressures.

In 1984–85 a research team of which I was a participant conducted an investigation on schoolchildren's attitudes towards work. Among other things, data from this research project showed that girls and boys still had very traditional views on what types of jobs they wanted to have when grown up. This came as a disappointment to the school administration, as much intervention work had been carried out in Norway in the 1970s in order to change these attitudes, and it was hoped that at least some changes had taken place during the early 1980s to reduce stereotyping of roles. It had also been expected that boys' and girls' attitudes to equality between the sexes would have become more flexible and more positive.

As a result of the above-mentioned data, the Director of Education in the County of Hordaland wanted to start a research project in which schools would provide an untraditional sex-role atmosphere from the children's first weeks in school. I was asked if I wanted to direct the research. An interdisciplinary research team of social scientists from the University of Bergen, of teachers from the Teachers' College of Bergen and of representatives of the county and central government administration, has worked with teachers in schools in a research project which combines traditional scientific approaches, an action research mode, and developmental research techniques.

The team worked in close contact with teachers who were to start teaching the first grade in the autumn of 1987. An invitation was sent out to teachers in the county of Hordaland (which is surrounding and including the city of Bergen). Fourteen teachers, among them two male teachers, agreed to join in the project and became members of the research team. We have held a number of seminars in order to develop the research project's various aims and methods.

Aims

The research team has had very tough discussions as to what should be the meaning of the concept 'equality' and how we are going to achieve the type of equality between the girls and boys which we want. Many of the participants of the research team found it fairly easy to discuss how valuable it is for girls to change some of their ideas and learn to behave less traditionally, for example to develop more typically male interaction patterns. Also there was agreement on the advisability of teaching girls to use tools and do various kinds of small repair work. But they found it far more controversial to suggest that equality might also imply changes in the boys' behaviour, in their ideas and in their interaction patterns.

Gradually, however, the attitudes of the research project participants changed in these respects. Through various types of information, the participants were made aware of recent research data from studies of kindergartens and classrooms which indicate that boys very often dominate the interaction, both between teachers and pupils, and between pupils. As a result of this, teachers come to know each boy as an individual and boys receive an education which is better fitted to their individual needs, while girls very often are treated as members of a group. At the same time the teachers appeared to find girls easier to deal with but less stimulating as pupils. In Scandinavia, especially in Denmark, educational researchers have looked more closely at girls' typical interaction patterns in the classroom and have shown these patterns to be more supporting, more democratic, and also fostering better group working styles than those of boys. Teachers in Danish high schools have seriously suggested that all education in the higher classes ought to be organised in small groups, because this is the best way to encourage girls to take part in interaction in school, at the same time producing an environment in which the boys also gain (Frimodt Møller, 1988).

As a result of these discussions, the research team was able to agree on some clear aims which stated that the teachers should work to create an atmosphere where the girls were given as much attention as the boys and encouraged to use their interpersonal abilities. Teachers would also work to ensure that girls learned to use tools and were taught to take part in some of the tougher games. At the same time, the boys should be encouraged to be responsible for the well-being of their class-mates and learn some of the more traditionally female activities. While it was not a goal to reduce the boys' vitality, the teachers were to try to channel the more vigorous boys' activities into friendly and unaggressive patterns.

Methodology

It was decided to have fourteen control classes, and to construct tests which would be carried out both in the research project classes and the control classes in the autumn of 1987, the spring of 1988 and again in the spring of 1990. The number of pupils in the fourteen project classes and the fourteen control classes varied between fifteen and twenty-five. The total sample in each category was 250 pupils. In Norway, pupils begin the first grade in primary school in the year of their seventh birthday. As part of the research design, measures were proposed which would firstly help to create a gender-neutral, non-stereotypic learning environment, and secondly, help to counteract known patterns of boys' or of girls' behaviour which reinforce sex-role stereotyping.

The learning environment was seen as needing both control and reconstruction on several levels: practical and physical; discourse and oral interaction; use of pictures, books and materials; and sociometric. As part of the preparatory training seminars, members of the research project had also discussed the fact that boys and girls do not form homogenous groups, and that many boys are as quiet as many of the girls, and that for these boys as well as for the girls, it was seen of importance that the most dominating of the boys were not allowed to control what was going on among the pupils in the classroom, and between the teachers and the pupils.

At the *practical* level, the research team decided to divide the classrooms into five workshops and the class into a corresponding number of groups. The workshops have included (a) 'Work with tools', e.g. hammers, saws, screwdrivers; (b) 'Learning technology', e.g. constructing with technical lego; (c) 'Learning handicrafts', e.g. sewing, weaving, embroidery; (d) 'Learning housework', e.g. preparing food, setting the table, doing the dishes; (e) 'Learning carework', e.g. making dolls, making clothes and beds for them, playing with them. At the seminars, the teachers have given reports on the various activities, and have been very helpful in sharing with each other their experience as to what are the main problems and what are good ways to solve them. They have also shared all their ideas about useful pedagogical measures.

At the *physical* level, the teachers would arrange games which ask for a certain amount of physical courage, trying to make the girls take as much part in these games as the boys. Research has shown that this is important, and also that if boys are to enjoy taking part in the more typical girls' activities, they will also need some time for training. The teachers would use their authority to create an atmosphere where it became natural for all the pupils to share in the various activities, and for traditional boys' activities to alternate with those that are more often preferred by girls.

The research team had also gathered a collection of gender-neutral pictures which showed situations where boys and girls participate in ways which provided good material for discussions on equality between the sexes. Furthermore, the teachers organised various types of plays centred on favourite Norwegian fairy tales which featured the heroes and heroines in unusual or nontraditional sex roles.

The control of *discourse* was seen as more difficult. Firstly the teachers agreed to make it one of their main efforts to try to avoid letting the more dominating among the boys take control over the interaction among the pupils inside and outside the classroom, being particularly aware of the patterns shown in many types of classroom research that when a teacher has started talking with a girl, very often a boy interrupts and takes over the interaction. The opposite pattern is very seldom found.

A set of tests were developed through which the research team has measured the children of the project—and the control classes when they started school in the autumn of 1987. The tests were based on drawings, since most of the children could not read or write. These tests were repeated in the spring of 1988, and some similar tests are to be developed and given in the spring of 1990 when the pupils are in the third grade. The team also constructed some very simple 'control sheets' for the teachers to use in order to record as they went along, which of the methods they used, how these methods worked, and general and special reactions from the pupils. Two of the researchers (an anthropologist with experience from kindergarten research and the writer and Project Director who have previous varied research experience), conducted series of observations in the classrooms and interviews of the teachers at various points during the research period.

Interim Results

Since the project is still in train, only interim results are available, but these already tend to confirm some hypotheses and raise interesting issues.

Based on the results of the tests presented to the research project classes and the control classes in the first weeks of school, and after six months, we found very clear general gender stereotypes as to the children's views on which activities girls and boys generally like and do not like. However, when the individual children indicated what types of activities they personally preferred or did not prefer, there was a less clear correspondence with these stereotypes, although there were still significant differences between the sexes in the expected directions. When presented with pictures of various types of jobs that the children may carry out at home, more girls consistently answered both that they did more of these jobs and that they did them more frequently. There were some differences as to how the children reacted to drawings of people who were in need of help: girls answered more often than boys that they would give help. We shall be working on a more sophisticated type of test to be used in the final year of the project.

Gender roles in use of simple tools and home skills

For the practical project work observed so far, the teachers reporting on the 'workshop corner' record that most of the girls have been very positive as to the learning of how to use ordinary tools; one girl for example saying: 'I had no idea that I was able to use a hammer'. For some of the more complicated activities, girls have needed more coaching than boys, and have showed a more timid attitude. However, most of the girls have become very interested, and some have shown remarkable technical ability even at this early age. Very few girls have complained that these were boys' activities and have shown little interest as a result.

Teachers reporting on 'the housework groups' record that both boys and girls have enjoyed making various types of meals. Some of the boys have become as interested as the girls in setting the table with bright napkins, some even bringing flowers they have picked themselves. When it comes to doing the dishes, a much greater number of the boys than the girls have little training, and have to learn the most basic facts like the difference in use of towels and dishcloths. Some of the boys have reacted very negatively, one boy asking the teacher if she really expected him to put his hands into that water . . . Some boys have also been anxious that children from other classes should *not* look in on them while they carried out this task. However, by and by most of the boys stopped arguing. As to learning how to sew, many more boys than girls needed coaching regarding how to use needle and thread. While most of the girls enjoyed this activity and could keep on working for a long time, the boys wanted to finish very quickly.

However, when allowed to use the sewing machine, many more boys became really interested. Some have even started using their mothers' machines at home.

Role playing for learning to care

Using play and role-play activities, we discovered that the greatest differences between boys and girls have been observed—not unexpectedly—in connection with the making of dolls and playing with them. *In the beginning, some of the boys treated their dolls very brutally. They had to be taught how to carry them.* But after a while most of the boys started to like this type of activity. Some made their dolls look like Superman, or made cowboy clothes for them. Other boys became very interested in the care of the dolls, and a few insisted on taking their dolls home for Christmas so that they should not be alone in the schoolroom.

Discussions in the classroom and dramatisation

Many of the teachers have found it very effective to use situations from the housework and doll playing as a basis for discussions and dramatisation, in order to work with the stereotyped attitudes on sex roles that appeared during these sessions. Some of the teachers have found dilemmas in handling the information about the sex-role patterns to which the children themselves impulsively refer when reflecting about the sex-role patterns of their own families, for example the boy who said that the only times his father did any shopping were when he lacked cigarettes . . .

Gender and physical activity

Many of the boys have needed training in order to be able to play hopscotch, but have liked it very much when they have mastered this activity. However, all of the teachers find that the boys are most intensely interested in playing football. Some of the girls also like this, but most of the girls get tired sooner than the boys. It is very difficult to make the boys give up a football game for another type of activity when the girls don't want to play football any more. Many of the teachers report that boys are also very reluctant to take a girl by the hand if the class is to form a ring. It seems that in these physical activity situations more often than in any of the others, the teachers have had to use their authority in order to create situations that are as rewarding for the girls as for the boys. Some of the teachers report rather bitter comments from the girls from these types of situations as to the unfairness of the boys' attitudes.

Common findings across ability ranges

Many of the teachers report that in the various practical activities, the differences between the pupils with higher and lower abilities for schoolwork seem to disappear. The teachers think this is because the tasks are of a practical nature, and after a certain amount of training, all the pupils have been able to carry them out. Also, most of the pupils have developed great interest in the various activities, and the teachers argue that this is because they combine aspects both of play and of meaningful work.

Some preliminary results from observations in the second year

The teachers' reports on the girls' abilities as to using ordinary tools, using technical lego and solving other technical problems are confirmed. We have been very impressed both regarding the girls' degree of ability and engagement. Concerning the boys' activities in the housework workshops, they have different patterns from those of girls—they are less neat, and they clearly have less training—but most of them show a very high degree of interest in cooking and somehow they manage to produce edible food. They use more energy doing the dishes and cleaning up, but most of them do it without withdrawing from the job, and some even seem to like it. As to care work, we might place what we saw of the boys' patterns on a continuum: a small number reacted negatively, some showed little interest, many were carrying out the activities in a satisfactory manner—and quite a few were very enthusiastic.

We were highly impressed by the children's ability to work independently. In the beginning of each workshop, each group was given a written workplan by the teachers. They read it together and then set to work. They were given some advice by the teachers, but were to a great degree able to manage on their own. We observed a few examples of negative interaction patterns both in girls' and in boys' groups, and in mixed groups, but most of the groups were working very well together.

Some preliminary results from the interviews with the teachers in the second year

All the teachers maintained that they saw the project as very important both regarding the children and themselves. To take part had been a great challenge and meant a lot of hard work, but they did not regret having agreed to join the project.

All of them found that they had become much more observant as to traditional sex-role patterns and engaged in changing them. Most of the teachers also reported that they had learned important new pedagogic techniques.

Regarding the plans for the third year, the research team has worked together in order to develop new tasks for the carework workshop. The teachers plan to invite children from nearby kindergartens, and also to visit homes for the elderly. Furthermore, the classes will adopt pupils from first-year classes.

Teachers and parents

As part of the action research approach, one of the aims of the research team has been to enlist the help of the parents in the work for greater equality between the sexes in the classrooms. Some of the parents have been active in getting together material for the workshop corner. All the parents have reacted positively when asked to control that the job is done whenever the children are given as homework to make their own bed, do the dishes, clean a floor etc. As far as the teachers have been able to observe, none of the parents has been negative towards the project.

There have been, inevitably, variations in the teachers' handling of classroom situations. The situation for the teachers as to resources is not homogenous: some of the municipalities have been willing to give more resources than others, both as to assistant teachers and material resources. Some of the teachers, for example, also have severely handicapped pupils integrated in their classes, again with differences as to allocation of appropriate resources. But even if some of the teachers clearly are having to tackle very difficult situations, they have not left the project.

We have continued the seminars as part of the interdisciplinary action research approach. In the seminars there is a continuing discussion among the teachers as to how much of their teaching should be influenced by their taking part in the project. Some of the teachers set aside a certain number of lessons for the project's various pedagogical measures, others do not clearly distinguish between project procedures and ordinary teaching; all of their activities are influenced by the ideas behind the project. The research team has developed no clear rules about to which degree the teachers carry out the various project activities in mixed or in single sex groups, preferring to evaluate the different approaches. As to both these questions of teacher behaviour, the results of the classroom observations and teachers' interviews which were carried out in the second year of the project, are expected to provide a basis for more homogenous procedures in the third year, and later reports will deal with this.

The research team intends to produce a 'Handbook for Teachers in Sex Role Education' in which the teachers taking part in the project will share with other teachers and teachers' college students, their various types of experience and give detailed descriptions of the activities in the workshops.

Conclusion

Research is still continuing, but it is useful to report even at the interim stage, some general trends that are confirmed, as well as detailed results. In general, we can report that

- Even in their *first weeks of formal schooling*, very clear gender stereotypes occur on what activities in the classroom are liked and are 'acceptable' to each sex.
- At this early stage, evidence emerges of gender sterotyping of tasks in the home.
- Even at this young age, in almost all observed practices girls were more willing to move away from stereotyped roles or to adjust, than boys. Boys' attitudes to change and to doing 'nontraditional' activities were consistently more negative.
- Boys had more difficulty with the everyday tasks they saw as 'female' (mainly to do with home and children), than the reverse. They needed more coaching.
- Notwithstanding, there are encouraging signs that counteractive strategies and control of the learning environment do help to make tasks and activities more gender neutral.

In summary, while we find, as data from other types of research on sex-role behaviour also show, that both boys' attitudes towards traditional female activities and their typically male behaviour patterns are more difficult to change than those of girls, the teachers and observers do report some important tendencies which we hope will become stronger in the third year.

References

Frimodt Møller, Inger (1988) *Paedagogik og pigers selvverd i gymnasiet I: Seminar-rapport Piger i Kvindefag.* Copenhagen: Arbejds Direcktoratet.

AUSTRALIAN RESEARCH ON GENDER IN EDUCATION

Shirley N. Sampson

Faculty of Education, Monash University, Clayton, VIC 3168, Australia

Abstract   A range of Australian research concerned with gender in education is reviewed. Despite an increased research investment into issues of schooling, vocational education, teacher–student interaction and innovative action research, schooling is slow to change its gender bias. Some Australian research does not, however, replicate European findings.

Apart from some interest in sex differences in earlier years, research into gender in education is a product only of the last twenty-five years or less, in most countries. As issues to do with women's role have increased in importance in Australia, so too has the field of research into gender or socially created differences in the education of girls and women, boys or men, with most interest centred on the education of females. There is widespread acceptance that boys' problem behaviour in primary school and early reading difficulties are socially engendered, but relatively little research attention has been accorded to these phenomena except in one instance referred to below.

Since the early 1970s when evidence still only consisted of sweeping assertions, often poorly documented, about girls' disadvantages in participation, achievements and outcomes of schooling compared with boys, awareness has become more widespread, beginning first with demands for the collection and publication of statistics concerning female compared with male participation and achievement in education. Increasing pressures from parents, feminists and others that their daughters should not be as disadvantaged by their schooling as they clearly were, have led to a progressively more accurate, researched body of knowledge as information became more readily available. Legislation requiring public accountability for equality of opportunity has now ensured the publication of most educational statistics in a form which illustrates the relative position of both sexes. In this paper, I hope to show the direction of the principal trends in the subsequent more exact research within the context of Australian schools and systems and concentrating on the decade of the 1980s.

Legislation and action directed towards equal opportunity for girls in schools has been enacted in most Australian States and federally in the years since 1974. Equal Opportunity consultants were appointed in Education Ministries and have been able to make some inroads into structural inequalities such as access and funding, although it is argued that in the course of becoming servants of the bureaucracy, these officers have become less powerful and thus less able to make basic changes to the system itself (Franzway *et al.*, 1989). Certainly the mere equal provision of *opportunity* which is now available has been insufficient radically to alter teachers' expectations and girls' patterns of schooling.

Youth unemployment which has been much higher for girls, coupled with national requirements for economic reorganisation during the early 1980s, made it urgent for schools to contribute to workforce restructuring. In 1987, this led to a National Policy for the Education of Girls adopted with the consent of all States, based upon the principle of taking affirmative action during the period of compulsory education in order to produce changes in outcomes for girls and women in employment, earning capacity and share of leadership roles.

Following a massive influx of married women to the workforce in the 1960s in Australia, secondary education provided for girls was geared to produce the skills required for a work role in a highly segregated, lowly paid and often part-time female workforce in which two thirds of all women employees worked in clerical, sales and service occupations, a process analysed in some detail by O'Donnell (1984). Pressures from escalating social changes such as declining marriage rates, reduction in family size and from 1976, an increasing divorce rate have left many women as sole income earners for themselves and their children over the same period as the value of female-dominated areas of work has been dramatically reduced by the introduction of new technologies. Demand has risen for new technical skills, for which, in Australia, girls are poorly equipped to undertake training, as a result of voluntarily opting out of some prerequisite studies or introductory skills subjects normally taught in schools; and also as a consequence of a particularly stereotyped view of appropriate female work. As a consequence, despite official insistence on change, there are few female students in technical college courses (Sweet, 1982, 1983; Pocock, 1988) or in combined school/apprenticeship courses other than hairdressing. In the metal, building, vehicle and electrical trades, for instance, female apprentices constitute only 0.7%, 1.3%, 0.9% and 1.6% respectively of all apprentices, Australia wide (National Data Base, 1988).

In line with these social and economic trends, research and evaluation of girls' school experiences has come to focus much more closely on changing girls' educational choices, both directly and by indirect means in order to provide more options for entry to a wider range of training and to ensure more financial independence for adult women (Yates, 1985). Detailed analysis of dysfunctional female work patterns (Game & Pringle, 1983) has shown how school practice and curriculum reinforce gender stereotypes present in the wider society by, for example, legitimating the expenditure of school time on shorthand and typing, rather than more office technology, or by the place accorded to home economics as 'caring for the family' rather than as a preparation for work in the tourist industry or food trades and by the subtle gender differentiation between the sexes which appears in school timetables and organisation and other aspects of the hidden curriculum (Taylor, 1982; Porter, 1986; Connell et al., 1982). Sociologists have shown how patriarchal values about work and the home and the care of children are reproduced through schooling and the social control of entry to the workforce and of work practices (Connell, 1987; O'Donnell & Hall, 1988).

The role of teachers in mediating such values has constituted a major feature of research and writing on gender and education in the last decade in Australia. While girls' choice of future occupation has been shown to result from stereotyped expectations on the part of teachers and those whose role it is to organise timetable and curriculum offerings, these factors are accepted because they fit in with parents' own experiences and assumptions (Earley, 1981; Currie, 1982; Saha, 1982; Trotman, 1984). Discerning analysis has traced the way in which adults, both parents and teachers who are connected to primary schools add their particular weight to the 'gender agenda' which children experience (Evans, 1988) and manage to create division between the sexes from earliest schooling (Clark, 1989). Teachers who are such an important part of the school experience, although espousing more equal roles for their pupils, have been shown to actually live out very conservative gender roles, themselves (Evans, 1982). In the secondary school, the interaction of the same conservative forces with the additional influence of a powerful peer group has been amply illustrated (Connell *et al.*, 1982).

Concern with sex differences in post-secondary education and the sex-segregated workforce has focused on the subject choices of both girls and boys during school years, and particularly on the failure of girls to select subjects from a range of physical sciences or continuing and advanced mathematics. There are marked State variations in subject participation at all levels (e.g. only 8% of girls in the final year of school study physics in Victoria, compared with 16.2% in South Australia). Although they do not enter technical or mathematical/scientific studies in equal numbers at tertiary levels, it seems anomalous that females participate in greater numbers in science and maths than in languages and history until year 12, when the situation is reversed and at the highest level of maths and in physical sciences, their participation rate is well below males (National Data Base, 1988).

Research has been directed towards the content and process of these curricula, demonstrating the masculinity of their orientation (Carss, 1981)—but also how they may be made intrinsically more interesting and relevant to both sexes (McLintock Collective, 1989b). Some researchers have focused on the characteristics of the students, trying to evaluate the influence of different levels of spatial ability (Wattanawaha & Clements, 1982; Willis, 1980). Other work has shown that in their mid-teens bright girls display a little more fear of success (Leder, 1982) and that many girls attribute success and failure to factors outside their control (Leder, 1984). However, it is the apparent lack of career relevance of scientific and mathematical studies to girls, to the stereotyped work roles which women are still seen performing, which has been shown to be of overriding importance (Morgan, 1979; Brown & Fitzpatrick, 1981; Earley, 1981; Jones, 1981; Naylor, 1984).

The contribution of the teacher has been found to be biased in favour of boys in these and other subjects in recognition of creativity (Evans, 1979) and in the use of scientific and mathematical competence as evidence of the value of the person (Fomin, 1984). The questioning practices used by teachers have been shown to demonstrate hidden assumptions about pupil competence, with boys expected to evidence more ability to abstract and apply what they learn (Leder, 1989). The sex of the teacher also appears to act as a possible role model for both sexes, with women teachers improving girls' performance in mathematics and male teachers encouraging boys in reading skills (Schofield, 1982, 1983).

Whilst there has consistently been a higher retention rate of females than males to the final years of schooling since the 1970s, women reached 51% of higher education students in 1988, nationwide. Despite this increasing participation, however, they are heavily concentrated in Arts faculties, and in teacher preparation courses, with males greatly predominating in the Technical and Further Education sector where women cluster in hairdressing and to a lesser extent in food and printing trades. Females are less likely to be studying at all ages after compulsory years or as part of their employment (Office of the Status of Women, 1989; National Data Base, 1988).

Yates (1987) has noted what appears to be a greater volume of action research or decentralised school-based activities undertaken in Australia in comparison with England and the United States. This may well be a consequence of the centralised tax system which has left the Federal government without the responsibility for the basic provision of schooling, but being the only authority with funds available for innovation. Certainly the major source of funds for research in education in the last decade has been the Federally initiated and funded Commonwealth Schools Commission and the Federal Ministry. Whilst powerless to radically alter the conduct of schooling, these two bodies have provided funds for schools or teachers who are willing to undertake local initiatives. In the case of the education of girls, these have included, *inter alia*, a three-year action study of a group of schools trying to increase girls' physical activity (Oldenove, 1989), and action to increase girls' retention in a remote rural area (see Martinez *et al.*, in Leder & Sampson, 1989) as well as a multitude of smaller projects such as the provision of transport for girls to attend a nearby technical school, focused professional development for teachers and parents, the publication and dissemination of results from specific programmes; and also updating statistics about all aspects of women's and girls' education (National Data Base, 1988). Some of these initiatives to change girls' choices have been evaluated (Kennedy, 1981; Sampson, 1983; Foster, 1984; Leder & Sampson, 1989). There is, however, evidence of only slow and sporadic adoption of such insights into mainstream schooling (Willis & Kenway, 1986). Resistance to the intervention of the Federal government in state-controlled schooling even by such injection of funds is still evident; and as a consequence, action research tends to remain localised and few of the findings have been widely publicised.

Although girls' school participation in higher level mathematics and the study of the physical sciences has improved only slowly over the decade, there has been little attempt to put into practice, at pre-service level, aspects of teacher training which have been shown to increase effectiveness in developing primary teachers' interest and involvement in science (Rennie, Parker & Hutchinson, 1985) or offering practical activities for post-primary teachers (Barnes *et al.*, 1984). Christensen & Massie (1989) have illustrated the circular process of reproduction of less than exciting teaching in this subject, while a recent report to the Federal education authority has emphasised the distance which tertiary institutions have to travel still, in order to become even as innovative as the school system in enlarging teachers' skills in teaching all the sciences (DEET, 1989). In a comparative study with Thailand, Australian researchers have shown that the kind of gendered choices we have here in subjects such as senior school chemistry and physics can be completely reversed with different social expectations for girls (Klainin, Fensham & West, 1987) but, as yet, there has been little attempt of any kind at tertiary level to reverse the trend.

An important stream of research in Australia was fuelled, in 1973, by renewed Federal funding for non-government schools, most of which were originally for one sex only. Its focus has been into the advantages and disadvantages for girls of being educated in single-sex or coeducational schools. Many single-sex schools, mostly boys' schools, have sought to increase their numbers and thus the variety of subjects offered, by taking in the opposite sex. As well, most of the small number of older government schools which are single-sex have needed to amalgamate as urban populations have moved. This has led to a stream of research seeking to justify these changes and to establish advantages in terms of achievement, participation in a wider range of studies, or generally, social benefits from educating the sexes together. It has been demonstrated conclusively that the achievement of both sexes does not vary significantly under either arrangement (Carpenter, 1985; Rowe, 1988; Marsh et al., 1989) and that the majority prefer to be educated together largely for social reasons (Harris, 1986). Some girls have been found to be happier when studying 'male stereotyped' subjects without boys and other studies have focused on school and classroom climate or teacher attention to boys, in order to show that coeducation has disadvantages for girls as a consequence of boys' behaviours in quelling girls' spontaneity (Gill, 1988; Sampson, 1989). Other research has reviewed a combination of factors to do with male notions of 'ownership' of some hitherto mainly male studies and the fact that, with both boys and girls together in a class, teachers appear to be unable to accord to girls the assistance and affirmation of individual abilities which they have no difficulty conveying to boys in classes such as mathematics and sciences, technical studies, economics, etc. (Jones, Kyle & Black, 1987; Leder, 1987). There has been little evaluative conclusion, but much small-scale action research to see if these factors can be alleviated by the provision of single-sex classes for girls for particular subjects or age levels (Gill, 1988).

Many areas of curriculum have been studied in terms of their gender bias within this decade (Foster, 1989). These have included the use of language in schools, both written and spoken, showing how gender roles are constructed (Ramsay, 1983; Freebody & Baker, 1987). Omission of women from the discourse has been explored with regard to the teaching of Australian history and the history of the education of women (Williamson, 1980; Windschuttle, 1980; MacKinnon, 1984; Theobald, 1984; Jones, 1985; Kyle, 1986; Taylor & Henry, 1989).

Physical Education and Sports have been shown to have a male bias, but research has illustrated how important this participation is for raising girls' self esteem (Coles, 1979; Dyer, 1982, 1986) and, as mentioned earlier, a major action research project attempting to increase girls' involvement has been successfully implemented and evaluated in a large number of schools in one State (Oldenove, 1989).

Analysis of education about sexuality in Australian schools has documented another major aspect of gender bias, with boys learning an instrumental attitude to relationships while girls continue to expect great personal commitment from their partners (Szirom, 1988). The school's role in the reproduction of these differences between the sexes was originally demonstrated by McCarthy (1983) and provided the basis for a widely acclaimed publication describing curriculum action for schools (Clarity Collective, 1982).

As a consequence of the diversity of origins of children in Australian schools, gender differences for migrant populations have been analysed, showing that some populations, notably some European and Asian born, actually have a higher proportion of females studying scientific and technical subjects than the Australian born. On the other hand there are enormous variations between them (Foster & Stockley, 1984; Foster, 1988). In higher education, Powles (1987) has revealed that despite difficulties experienced by some migrant groups, mostly recent migrants of Middle Eastern origin, generally speaking, girls do not appear to be disadvantaged. The daughters of fathers born outside Australia complete degrees in greater proportions than do daughters of Australian born fathers. Aborigines as an ethnic

group have been shown to be much less fortunate (Gale *et al.*, 1987) with
social dislocation being a much more important factor than gender differences in
education.

Apart from research into gender issues in schooling itself, a major field of study
which has emerged recently has focused on education as a workplace for women.
Research has outlined the history of women's position as teachers (Williamson,
1983; Spaull, 1989), their aspirations (Wentworth, 1979), the terms of their
employment (1984) and their disadvantage in the promotion stakes (Nash &
Sungaila, 1984; Sampson, 1987a, 1987b, 1989). As employees in the tertiary
system, the situation with regard to women is a little different from that in schools
(where women are some 60% of all employees). In universities, colleges and
technical and further education, women constitute a very small proportion of
employees with tenured or senior positions (Gale, 1980; Craney & O'Donnell,
1983; Cass *et al.*, 1983; Reilly, 1984); and this proportion has been found to
increase at a much slower rate than for other employment systems such as the
various State and Commonwealth public services (Allen, 1986). Research has so
far failed to explain this phenomenon satisfactorily (Over & Lancaster, 1984).

As a consequence of disadvantage suffered in earlier, more restrictive areas of
schooling, large numbers of mature-age women, many with family responsibilities,
have re-entered education since the mid seventies. Research has shown that their
achievements, overall, surpass those of younger students and, far from being a
middle class hobby group, as they are sometimes depicted, the majority have
entered the workforce upon graduation, thereby avoiding the poverty traps following divorce or sole parenthood which have befallen many of their generation
(Currie *et al.*, 1984; Burns, 1984; Kelly, 1987; Martin, 1987). Analysis of the
participation of this group of women has shown that their numbers are now
declining as a consequence of a government decision to re-introduce student fees
(AVCC, 1989).

Whilst a number of earlier studies demonstrating qualitative or quantitative
differences between females and males in education in Australia have necessarily
been omitted from this brief overview of research in the last ten years, the main
trends have been highlighted as well as the social circumstances in which each
has emerged. With a continuing heavy dependence of the Australian research
establishment on governmental sources of fundings, this link between social need
and funded research or evaluation is likely to continue. Some issues which will
remain in focus (or may re-emerge) in the near future would appear to be research
into gender differences in participation in higher education among disadvantaged
groups as a consequence of the re-introduction of fees; more discipline-initiated
and oriented evaluation of the curriculum, particularly in technological studies
and the physical sciences; teacher education and teacher influence on the participation of girls and women in science and technology studies at all levels; a much
more stringent analysis of the effectiveness of single-sex or coeducational school
or class settings for girls' attitudes, aspirations and achievements, as well as a
more focused evaluation of projects expanding girls' subject choices and career
options. It is to be anticipated, I believe, that future gender research will be used
to suggest answers to some of the problematic outcomes of schooling for each
sex, rather than to further illustrate the extent of sex differences. There appears
to be no indication, as yet, that the field of gender research will falter for want
of topics to study, or the willingness of academics and others to investigate such
issues.

References

Allen, F. (1986) Progress or stagnation. University of Melbourne, 1974–1984. Unpublished doctoral dissertation, Monash University, Clayton, Victoria.

AVCC Australian Vice Chancellor's Committee (1989). Press release, May 15.

Barnes M., Plaister, R. and Thomas, A. (1984) *Girls Count in Mathematics and Science: A Handbook for Teachers*. Darlinghurst: Mathematical Association of NSW.

Brown, S. and Fitzpatrick J. (1981) Girls, boys and subject choice. Discussion Paper No. 11, Research Branch, Education Department, Perth.

Burns, R. (1984) Getting there, staying on. In R. Burns and B. Sheehan (eds) *Women and Education*. Bundoora: La Trobe University Press.

Carpenter, P. (1985) Single-sex schooling and girls' academic achievements. *Australia and New Zealand Journal of Sociology* 21, 3, 456–72.

Carss, M. (1981) Girls and mathematics—What did you say? *Research in Mathematics Education* 2, 68–81.

Cass, B., Dawson, M., Temple, D., Wills, S., and Winkler, A. (1983) *Why So Few? Women Academics in Australian Universities*. Sydney: Sydney University Press.

Christensen, C. and Massey, D. (1989, forthcoming). Perpetuating gender inequity: Attitudes of teacher education students. *Australian Journal of Education*.

Clarity Collective (1982). *Taught Not Caught: Strategies for Sexuality Education*. Melbourne: Spiral.

Clark, M. (1989) *The Great Divide: The Construction of Gender in the Primary School*. Canberra: Curriculum Development Centre.

Coles, E. (1979) *Sport in Schools: The Participation of Girls*. Sydney: NSW Education Department Social Development Unit.

Connell, R. W., Ashenden, D. J., Kessler, S. and Dowsett, G. (1982) *Making the Difference: Schools, Family and Social Division*. Sydney: Allen & Unwin.

—— (1987) *Gender and Power*. Sydney: Allen & Unwin.

Craney, J. and O'Donnell, C. (1983) Women in advanced education: Advancement for whom? *Higher Education Research and Development* 2, 2, 129–46.

Currie, J. (1982) The sex factor in occupational choice. *Australian and New Zealand Journal of Sociology* 18, 2, 180–95.

Currie, J., Baldock, C., Murray, M. and Bossing, G. (1984) Mature age students. Murdoch University Report No. 1, Perth.

Department of Employment, Education & Training (DEET) (1989) *Report of the National Disciplinary Review of Mathematics and Science Teacher Education*. Canberra: DEET.

Dyer, K. (1982) *Challenging the Men: The Social Biology of Female Sporting Achievement*. St Lucia: University of Queensland Press.

—— (1986) Girls, physical education and self esteem: A review of research, resources & strategies. Report to the Commonwealth Schools Commission, Canberra.

Earley, P. D. (1981) Girls, school and work: Technological change and female entry into non-traditional work areas. *Australian Journal of Education* 25, 3, 269–87.

Evans, T. (1979) Creativity, sex role socialisation and pupil–teacher interaction in early schooling. *The Sociological Review* 27, 1, 139–55.

—— (1982) Being and becoming: Teachers' perceptions of sex-roles and actions toward their male and female pupils. *British Journal of Sociology of Education* 3, 2, 127–44.

—— (1988) *The Gender Agenda*. Sydney: Allen & Unwin.

Fomin, F. (1984) The best and the brightest—The selective function of mathematics in the school curriculum. In L. Johnson and D. Tyler (eds) *Cultural Politics*. Melbourne: Melbourne University Working Papers No. 5.

Foster, L. (1988) *Diversity and Multicultural Education: A Sociological Perspective*. Sydney: Allen & Unwin.

Foster, L. and Stockley, D. (1984) *Multiculturalism: The Changing Australian Paradigm*. Clevedon: Multilingual Matters.

Foster, V. (1984) *Changing Choices: Girls, School and Work*. Sydney: Hall & Iremonger.

—— (1989) Is 'gender-inclusive' curriculum the answer for girls? In G. Leder and S. Sampson *Educating Girls: Practice and Research*. Sydney: Allen & Unwin.

Franzway, S., Court, D. and Connell, R. W. (1989) *Staking a Claim: Feminism, Bureaucracy and the State*. Sydney: Allen & Unwin.

Freebody, P. and Baker, C. (1987) The construction and operation of gender in children's first books. In A. Pauwels (ed.) *Women and Language in Australian and New Zealand Society*. Sydney: Australian Professional Publications.

Gale, F. (1980) Academic staffing: The search for excellence. *Vestes* 23, 1, 3–8.

Gale F., Jordan, D., McGill, G., McNamara, N. and Scott, C. (1987) Aboriginal Education. In J.
    Keeves (ed.) *Australian Education: Review of Recent Research.* Sydney: Allen & Unwin.
Game, A. and Pringle, R. (1983) *Gender at Work.* Sydney: Allen & Unwin.
Gill, J. (1988) *Which Way to School.* Canberra: Commonwealth Schools Commission.
Harris, M. (1986) Coeducation and sex roles. *Australian Journal of Education* 30, 2, 117–31.
Jones, G. (1981) Why students drop out of mathematics—A conceptual framework for research.
    Research in Mathematics Education in Australia 1, 128–35.
Jones, H. (1985) *Nothing Seemed Impossible: Women's Education & Social Change in South Australia
    1875–1915.* St Lucia: University of Queensland Press.
Jones, J., Kyle, N. and Black, J. (1987) The tidy classroom: An assessment of the change from single
    sex to coeducation in New South Wales. *Australian Journal of Education* 31, 3, 284–302.
Kelly, S. (1987) *The Prize and the Price: The Changing World of Women Who Return to Study.* Sydney:
    Methuen Haynes.
Kennedy, R. (ed.) (1981) *Expanding the Options—Girls, Mathematics and Employment.* Sydney: Social
    Development Unit, Ministry of Education.
Klainin, S., Fensham, P. and West, L. (1987) Learning achievement in Upper Secondary School
    chemistry in Thailand: Some remarkable sex reversals. *International Journal of Science Education*
    9/2, 217–27.
Kyle, N. (1986) *Her Natural Destiny: The Education of Women in New South Wales.* Sydney: University
    of New South Wales Press.
Leder, G. (1982) Mathematics achievement and fear of success. *Journal for Research in Mathematics
    Education* 3, 2, 124–35.
—— (1984) Sex differences in attributions of success and failure. *Psychological Report* 54, 57–8.
—— (1987) Teacher–student interaction: A case study. *Education Studies in Mathematics* 18, 255–71.
—— (1989) Do girls count in mathematics? In G. Leder and S. Sampson *Educating Girls: Practice
    and Research.* Sydney: Allen & Unwin.
Leder, G. and Sampson, S. (1989) *Educating Girls: Practice & Research.* Sydney: Allen & Unwin.
McCarthy, W. (ed.) (1983) *Teaching About Sex: The Australian Experience.* Sydney: Allen & Unwin.
McKinnon, A. (1984) *One Foot on the Ladder: Origins and Outcomes of Girls' Secondary Schooling in
    South Australia.* St Lucia: University of Queensland Press.
McLintock Collective (1989) *Getting into Gear: Gender Inclusive Strategies in Science.* Canberra:
    Curriculum Development Centre.
Marsh, H., Owens, L., Marsh, M. and Smith, I. (1989) From single sex to coed schools. In G. Leder
    and S. Sampson (eds) *Educating Girls: Practice and Research.* Sydney: Allen & Unwin.
Martin, J. (1987) *Second Chance.* Ringwood: Penguin.
Morgan, C. (1979) Girls, boys and the decision to study eleventh grade non-terminal mathematics.
    Research in Mathematics Education 2, 85–99.
Nash, J. and Sungaila, H. (1984) Through the door marked 'Men Only'. In R. Burns and B. Sheehan
    (eds) *Women and Education.* Bundoora: La Trobe University Press.
National Data Base on the Education of Girls in Australia (1988) Sydney: NSW Ministry of Education
    and Youth Affairs.
Naylor, F. D. (1984) Sex, schools and emerging occupational interests. In I. Palmer (ed.) *Melbourne
    Studies in Education.* Melbourne: Melbourne University Press.
O'Donnell, C. (1984) *The Basis of the Bargain: Gender, Schooling and Jobs.* Sydney: Allen & Unwin.
O'Donnell, C. and Hall, P. (1988) *Getting Equal: Labour Market Regulation and Women's Work.*
    Sydney: Allen & Unwin.
Office of the Status of Women (1989) *National Agenda for Women: Implementation Report.* Canberra:
    Department of the Prime Minister and Cabinet.
Oldenove, H. (1989) Girls, P.E. and Sports. In G. Leder and S. Sampson (eds) *Educating Girls:
    Practice & Research.* Sydney: Allen & Unwin.
Over, R. and Lancaster, S. (1984) Career patterns in Australian universities. *Australian Journal of
    Education* 28, 3, 309–18.
Pocock, B. (1988) *Demanding Skill.* Sydney: Allen & Unwin.
Porter, P. (1986) *Gender and Education.* Deakin University: Deakin University Press.
Powles, M. (1987) *Women's Participation in Tertiary Education: A Review of Recent Australian Research*
    (2nd edn). University of Melbourne: Centre for the Study of Higher Education.
Ramsay, E. (1983) Language, politics and sexism in the classroom. *Education News* 18.
Reilly, S. (1984) Gender divisions in the academic workplace. In R. Burns and B. Sheehan (eds)
    Women and Education. Bundoora: La Trobe University Press.
Rennie, L., Parker, L. and Hutchinson, P. (1985) *The Effect of In-Service Training on Teacher Attitudes
    and Primary School Classroom Climate.* Perth: University of Western Australia Department of
    Education.

Rowe, K.J. (1988) Single-sex and mixed-sex classes: The effects of class type, student achievement, confidence and participation in mathematics. *Australian Journal of Education* 32, 2, 180–202.

Saha, L. (1982) Gender, school attainment and occupational plans: Determinants of aspirations and expectations among Australian urban school leavers. *Australian Journal of Education* 26, 3, 247–65.

Sampson, S. (1983) *Initiatives to Change Girls' Perceptions of Career Opportunities: An Evaluation.* Canberra: Australian Government Publishing Service.

—— (1987a) Equal opportunity alone is not enough or why there are more male principals in schools these days. *Australian Journal of Education* 31, 1, 27–42.

—— (1987b) But the women won't apply . . . *Unicorn* 13, 3, 139–43.

—— (1989) Are boys a barrier to girls in science? In G. Leder and S. Sampson *Educating Girls: Practice and Research.* Sydney: Allen & Unwin.

—— (forthcoming) Women teachers' careers? In P. McKenzie and R. MacLean *Australian Teachers' Careers.* Melbourne: ACER.

Schofield, H. (1982) Sex, grade level and the relationship between mathematics attitudes and achievement in children. *Journal of Educational Research* 75, 5, 280–4.

—— (1983) The development of sex differences in the preference for humanities or science-based courses: A retrospective study of tertiary students. *Collected Papers, Australian Association for Research in Education Conference, Canberra* (pp. 371–8).

Spaull, A (1989) Australian teachers' careers: An historical perspective. In P. McKenzie and R. MacLean *Australian Teachers' Careers.* Melbourne: ACER (forthcoming).

Sweet, R. (1982) *Some Indicators of Teenage Girls' Disadvantaged Labour Market Status.* Sydney: NSW Department of TAFE.

—— (1983) *An Analysis of the Australian Labour Market for Typists, Stenographers & Secretaries.* Sydney: NSW Department of TAFE.

Szirom, P. (1988) *Teaching Gender.* Sydney: Allen & Unwin.

Taylor, S. (1982) Schooling and social reproduction. *Australian Journal of Education* 26, 2.

—— (1984) Reproduction and contradictions in schooling: The case of commercial studies. *British Journal of Sociology of Education* 5, 1, 3–18.

Taylor, S. with Henry, M. (eds) (1989) *Battlers and Bluestockings: Women's Place in Australian Education.* Canberra: Australian College of Education.

Theobald, M. (1984) Mere accomplishments? Melbourne's early ladies' schools reconsidered. *History of Education Review* 13, 2, 15–28.

Trotman, J. (1984) Jobs for the girls: Family ideology and the employment of women in education. *Australian Journal of Education* 28, 2, 132–44.

Wattanawaha, N. and Clements, M. A. (1982) Qualitative aspects of sex-related differences in performance on pencil and paper spatial questions, Grades 7–9. *Journal of Educational Psychology* 74, 6.

Wentworth, R. (1979) Career aspirations of male and female teachers. *Journal of South Pacific Association of Teacher Education* 11, 3/4, 91–9.

Williamson, N. (1980) Factory to reformatory: The founding and failure of industrial and reform schools for girls in 19th century NSW. *Australian & New Zealand History of Education Society Journal* 9, 1 32–41.

—— (1983) The feminization of teaching in NSW: A historical perspective. *Australian Journal of Education* 27, 1, 33–44.

Willis, S. (1980) Sex differences in spatial ability: What can we do about them? In D. Williams and H. Crawford (eds) *Theory into Practice.* Canberra: Australian Association of Maths Teachers.

Willis, S. and Kenway, J. (1986) On overcoming sexism in schooling: To marginalise or mainstream? *Australian Journal of Education* 30, 2, 132–49.

Windschuttle, E. (ed.) (1980) *Women, Class and History.* Melbourne: Fontana/Collins.

Yates, L. (1985) Curriculum becomes our way of contradicting biology and culture: An outline of some dilemmas for non-sexist education. *Australian Journal of Education* 29, 1, 3–16.

—— (1987) Australian research on gender and education. In J. Keeves (ed.) *Australian Education: Review of Recent Research.* Sydney: Allen & Unwin.

WOMEN TEACHING IN EUROPEAN UNIVERSITIES: INTERVIEWS AND INFORMATION

Margaret B. Sutherland

46 The Scores, St Andrews, Fife KY16 9AS, Scotland

Abstract　This paper considers the strengths and weaknesses of the interview method in Comparative Education, especially when used in studying women who teach in universities. Results obtained in investigating the career perceptions of such women in different countries and common factors and differences in the circumstances of their careers, are presented and analysed.

Methods of Research in Comparative Education

In a world of increasingly greater international communication, knowledge of, and comparisons with, what happens in different educational systems become correspondingly important. We need to be aware of shared problems and other systems' ways of dealing with them. Although a great deal has been written and spoken about the methodology of Comparative Education, surprisingly little attention has been given to the use of common social science research techniques in this domain. Discussion has tended to centre on general principles, indeed on philosophical considerations of the nature of comparisons, the circumstances in which comparisons may be made, the determinist or other underlying assumptions, the possibilities of prediction (Schriewer & Holmes, 1988). Meanwhile, whatever the eventual outcome of such philosophical meditations, research in Comparative Education is somehow carried out. The methods most commonly used in practice are document analysis, comparisons of statistics, historical studies of the evolution of individual systems, case studies, or descriptive personal reporting. Occasionally more specialised document analyses concentrate on the literature of a chosen country or on school textbooks (UNESCO, 1982, 1983). Only rarely are objective—or fairly objective—tests of pupils' performance used, though the IEA studies have carried out such testing on an impressive scale (for example, IEA, 1988).

Analysis of existing data has much to commend it: obtaining new data by empirical studies is difficult when more than one educational system is involved. Apart from language complications (though some cross-cultural studies can be made in countries with a common language), there are travel costs and there may well be problems of access to schools and other educational institutions. Nevertheless, empirical research is worthwhile and as interviews are being increasingly used in other social science domains to elicit historical material or illuminate individual experiences it may be helpful to look initially, when reviewing findings about the position of women who teach in universities, at the strengths and weaknesses of the interview method in collecting data.

The investigations in question were to discover factors affecting the careers of women who teach in universities in different European countries—originally in France, Finland, East Germany, West Germany and Britain (Sutherland, 1985a, 1985b), then in a follow-up study, in Portugal. Initially, the questionnaire method was used as a preliminary to interviews, but although it proved helpful in some respects, with some groups, there were the usual problems of incomplete responses or failure to respond, and it did not seem possible to circulate—and get a reliable response to—questionnaires in various foreign countries.

Interviews proved to have various advantages. Firstly, while reasons for failure to respond to questionnaires are often obscure, reasons for the very few 'refusals' to be interviewed were given—they were always a matter of no suitable time being available. (This, of course, could be a polite excuse, masking other reactions: but the time arguments were most convincingly presented—e.g. the person approached was about to travel to a conference in South America; or the potential interviewee had special—stated—commitments which meant that she would not be able to meet the investigator until the week after the investigator's visit to her university city.) Secondly and more importantly, interviews let respondents add relevant points and allowed the investigator to put additional questions on points which proved more complex than expected.

There is of course a weakness associated with this flexibility of the interview. Respondents can introduce new and important aspects of the topic, but while this aspect can be included in subsequent interviews, it will be absent from earlier interviews. This means that data on the new aspect will be incomplete. But the findings from these interviews were not to be presented in statistical form or statistically analysed. So provided that all interviews included the major questions decided on at the beginning of the enquiry, data on these would be complete and other partial data could be reported with an indication of incompleteness. As some questions were open-ended, responses were in any case frequently unquantifiable.

Thirdly, interviews can reveal the differences between official statements and the actual experiences of those in an education system; they can also reveal details of normal practice in schools or other institutions, details considered too obvious or insignificant to be officially mentioned, but illuminating interpretations of the system. When, as in the investigations reported here, women of different age levels are interviewed, their experiences give insight into the evolution of the system, showing how changes affected successive generations of pupils and students. But to gain such advantages, all interviewing must be adequately prepared. In Comparative Education this means that it is necessary to know, before embarking on interviews, what the structure of the educational system of the country is, what examinations and qualifications are in operation, whether there have been recent changes and reforms. It is also important to know something of the history of the country in general, and its political structure. This background knowledge makes it much easier to comprehend what individuals say about their experiences and it saves wasting time while individuals expound the basic structures of schools and higher education institutions—though it can occasionally be useful to have knowledge of the system confirmed by such explanations.

Yet questions peculiar to Comparative Education arise with the matter of the language to be used in interviews. English-speakers have the great, and unfair, advantage that English is widely studied in Europe so that highly educated women—as in the groups studied—very often are competent in this language. Many indeed have studied in Britain or in the United States. This language competence of the people interviewed was essential in Finland and Portugal (though in the latter country French was sometimes an acceptable alternative). In France and the two Germanies, the home language or English was used as the woman interviewed preferred. A few women in Finland and Portugal brought along an 'interpreter', a colleague or student whom they considered more competent than themselves in English but this was not usually a happy solution, since dialogues between the woman interviewed and her interpreter seemed to be less than fully translated. Where the investigator is not competent in the foreign language there is the danger that the sample becomes biased towards women competent in English, or that answers given are misleading. Such language complications did not seem seriously to affect interviews now reported.

Finally, in interviews, there is the question of rapport. Being of the same sex and the same professional group as the people interviewed probably is advantageous. There is of course the associated danger of projection, assuming, for example, that the conditions of women's work in British universities are duplicated elsewhere: but interview data may spontaneously correct such misapprehensions, revealing, for instance, lack of contact between departments in foreign universities, and consequent lack of acquaintance with other women teachers. Projection could also mean bias in the choice of topic and the questions used. Topic choice is admittedly subjective, but the topic here chosen is widely studied and the main questions—'How did you come to be a university teacher?' 'How do you see your future career developing?' 'Why do you think this distribution of women at different ranks in university teaching occurs?'—were designed to be as neutral as possible. Interpretation of results, especially as carried out by only one person, could likewise be biased: hence care has been taken to report conflicting views— or simply to record without evaluation. Any omissions have been on the grounds of irrelevance or too small detail. Some indication of the reliability of the findings may be claimed from the correspondence between results found here and results reported by other researchers in the area (Heseltine, 1987; UNESCO, 1987; CEPES, 1988).

Observer effect was probably inevitable, the investigation changing subjects' perceptions of their situation, or at least increasing women's awareness of their status in university teaching, but this did not seem an undesirable effect. Some women were already feminist in outlook, some had not specially considered women's organisations though they were concerned for women's rights, others rejected feminism: increased awareness rather than bias seemed probable.

The interview method is time-consuming, especially in a single-handed investigation: it limits sample size. In fact, the numbers included are: 244 in the first investigation (in Britain, France, Finland, East Germany, West Germany) (Sutherland, 1985b) and 56 in the second investigation, in Portugal, which is reported in this article.

Interview Data from Portugal

Earlier research had shown the very different ways in which appointments to top levels of teaching in universities are made, and how women in different

European countries—Britain, Finland, France, East Germany, West Germany—perceive the career of university teaching and the situation of women in it. The research to be initially considered here attempted to answer, among others, the following questions: (a) How do women teaching in Portuguese universities perceive this career? (b) In Portuguese conditions, how is the 'dual role' of working women interpreted? (c) To what extent do findings from the Portuguese group support or contradict findings from interviews with women in other European countries—what is the general picture of the situation of women who teach in universities?

Women teaching in universities in Lisbon, Oporto, and Braga (University of Minho), were interviewed. They taught a wide range of subjects:

Biochemistry	1	Law	1
Biology, Botany, Genetics,		Medicine	2
Microbiology	7	Metallurgy	1
Chemistry	8	Pharmacy	1
Chemical Engineering	2	Philosophical Sciences	1
Economics	1	Physics	8
Education	11	Soc. Policy	1
English	8	Zoology	2
History	1		

They also represented different ranks in university teaching:

Assistants	16
Auxiliary Professors	14
Associate Professors	11
Professors with Chair	14
Secondary school teacher seconded to university teaching	1

The sample does not reflect the distribution of women at different levels in Portuguese universities since a deliberate effort was made to interview women professors (*catedráticos*) where possible. Although there has been a considerable increase in women teaching in universities during the past two decades, the overall percentages, in the three major university cities in 1984–85, were 40.6% at assistant level, 36.2% at auxiliary professor level, 26.5% at associate professor level, and 8.2% at the level of professor with Chair (Ruivo, 1985). It is interesting to contrast these figures with the proportions of women students in Portuguese universities: in 1985–85 women were 53% of those obtaining first degrees (CEPES, 1988).

Perceptions of the university teaching career

An important aspect of the career is the system of first appointment and subsequent promotions. Earlier research revealed considerable differences in making appointments in higher education in European countries. It can be argued that the more 'open' the system, the greater possibilities women have to advance in an academic career, for if various public examinations have to be taken and clearly stated conditions complied with, women have a clear objective. Women have been, until now, in a minority in this career: they have been less likely than men to benefit by informal contacts with senior university teachers, have had fewer role models, and very often have not thought about university teaching as a possible career for themselves or been perceived by senior male academics as having serious career prospects. Hence a system which clearly defines the qualifications needed at each stage, and which is 'open' in the sense of giving information as to availability of posts and as to how decisions are arrived at is helpful—men also may benefit by it. (Here it may be noted that in the Guidelines issued for institutions of higher education in Australia by the Affirmative Action Agency, review of appointing procedures is listed as a necessary step towards ensuring equal opportunities for women (AAA, 1987) and the Commission of the European Communities (1988), in more general Guidelines on 'positive action', has similarly advocated analysis of employment policies and of interviewing procedures.) On the other hand, when appointments depend largely on judgments based on personal impressions or confidential reports, greater scope is given for prejudices for or against women (or men in some categories) to operate.

Among systems studied, the United Kingdom has probably the least 'open' system, since the academic qualifications required at different levels are not rigidly defined: the doctorate's importance varies with subject area and according to level of employment—it is not stipulated as essential. The weight attached to 'outside' experience also varies from one discipline to another. Promotion from one level to the next depends on a number of factors, usually classified as research, teaching, administration and/or 'contribution to university, community or professional interests'. In practice, since teaching is difficult to evaluate objectively, assessment of research, judged normally by number of acceptable publications and/or amount of funding obtained, tends to play a dominant role. Willingness to undertake various administrative tasks may or may not improve the individual's chances of a high rating on the third aspect; similarly the role played in professional associations or in community activities outside the university may or may not be influential. In circumstances where the number of senior posts available is demonstrably insufficient, it is difficult for those under consideration for promotion to know whether justice has been done—and exactly how it has been done—though it can be regarded as progress towards 'openness' that many British universities have now allowed staff members to nominate themselves for consideration for promotion rather than wait to be proposed by their Professor or Head of Department. Similarly, for appointments at Chair level, research and publications—variously assessed—appear important, but other professional experience may count. And above all, there are still the confidential references or nominations, which seem likely to be subjective and differ in influence ('king-makers' still seem to exist for some disciplines and a candidate's prospects depend on whether or not the candidate has the right referees). There remains the equally subjective factor of the impression created at interview—though again, some recent appeals to tribunals have made appointing committees aware of the undesirability of putting biased questions to women. Differential payments to professors ('merit awards') are a further area of the career not open to public scrutiny.

In other European systems, the statement of qualifications is more explicit. The way to promotion lies through obtaining successive degrees and/or undergoing formal tests. France has a system of national committees to judge applicants for academic posts (thus trying to avoid local prejudices in appointing); in some disciplines it has the 'agrégation' examination, which includes an exacting oral, as well as written performance. France's highly demanding state doctorate degree has been the subject of considerable reform proposals during the last decade; the situation has been complicated by the introduction of the simpler doctorate of the third cycle and, in the last years, by the introduction of a new doctorate whose effectiveness remains to be established. But at the various stages, candidates for promotion at least know what the formal requirements are, even if personal factors (and members' characteristics) can still affect committees' deliberations.

Similarly, in West Germany there has been the recognised route of the first doctorate, followed by a later more important thesis leading, on examination, to Habilitation—being recognised as qualified to hold a Chair. Admittedly, the inrush of democracy following on the 1960s has meant that student opinion—after a trial lecture—has played some part in Chair appointments, and the role and nature of Habilitation have fluctuated, but again, the normal qualifying route has been clearly defined. In East Germany, likewise, Promotion A (a doctorate within a narrowly defined field) has to be followed by Promotion B (a doctorate of greater scope, with proof of competence in leading a research team, and with experience of academic work abroad) if a Chair is to be attained. And Finland has perhaps offered the most open of all systems with clear requirements not simply for doctoral qualifications but for published work which has to be submitted to named assessors, whose verdict in turn can be challenged.

What then is the situation in Portugal? Women, at the time of interview in 1987, proved to be well informed about what seemed a fairly open system. Portugal (despite some attempts to abolish discriminatory assessments in the euphoria of the years immediately following the 1974 revolution) has a clearly defined system of marks in academic examinations. Thus candidates for first appointment know whether they have a mark likely to put them high on the list of applicants—and know whether some other candidate appointed had indeed a higher mark. This system, it should be recognised, is new. Until the democratic reforms following the 1974 Revolution, first appointments were often—as in other European systems—at the disposal of Professors who could simply invite promising students to become assistants.

After this first appointment, there is a system of 'provas' or tests; the probationary assistant has to submit a record of work, pass an oral examination by department members, or give some evidence of mastership study, to become an established assistant. Then both men and women may benefit by the expansionist stage of Portuguese higher education. The country, having established a large number of new universities and polytechnics (Braga & Grilo, 1981), has been anxious to increase the number of people with doctoral degrees. A period of eight years has been allowed to the assistant to prepare the doctoral thesis, with the possibility of a year or more—up to three or four years, if the assistant studies abroad—free from teaching duties to concentrate on the research. If the doctorate is obtained, appointment as auxiliary professor follows.

Beyond this, the path of promotion remains clearly marked. Again, a public examination, and the quality of the curriculum vitae, lead to the rank of associate professor. Beyond that—after a generally agreed number of years—the agregação examination (again, a public examination based on the candidate's research work) leads to qualification for a Chair, though a vacancy has to be available before an actual appointment can be made.

From the interviews in Portugal it was clear that women were in no doubt what must be done if they wished to achieve promotion in the academic career.

It was also clear that the younger women, at the assistant level, were confident about their prospects. At this level—allowing for variations according to subject—they were about as numerous as men.

Beyond this level, however, there was rather less optimism. Although there is much openness in the system, there is also a fairly well established tradition of respect for seniority in the sense that a decent number of years is expected to elapse between one promotion and the next stage, and if a post in a department becomes available, it is recognised informally that there are some people whose 'turn' it is to apply. It is also recognised realistically that in some departments, given the recent expansion, senior posts are at present occupied by relatively young people (men, in the great majority of cases) so that the prospect of a vacancy is remote. As one woman put it, to get a Chair she'd have to kill off about half the department.

This in fact illustrates a point where European universities have different traditions about mobility between institutions. In Portugal the tradition has been for people to make their career within one university. It was indeed suggested by more than one person that 'outside' applicants would be looked upon with some degree of suspicion and that the internal candidates, being known in the university, were very likely to have priority. This situation of course may evolve now that there are many new universities. Formerly, Lisbon, Coimbra and Oporto were the only university cities: naturally people settled happily into working in these places where, often, they themselves had studied. Now that universities also exist in less important centres of population there could well develop a movement towards the longer established universities, as there has been for so long in France towards Paris. (In East Germany it is only in comparatively recent times that movement between universities has increased. West Germany, on the other hand, has not allowed Habilitation to take place—except in rare cases—in the university where a candidate was employed.) The British tradition has been for movement from one university to another, as has that of Finland: but in Britain mobility is being eroded by such factors as the present shortage of posts and the increase in short-term contracts.

Mobility in career terms has important implications for women who traditionally have moved with their husbands when the husband's career required a change of location, even if the woman's career was thus adversely affected. If, as often happens in other countries too, the Portuguese woman academic is married to a man who also teaches in higher education then the tradition of not changing universities helps to stabilise her career. But if her husband is not also in higher education, he may well have to move for career purposes, and she is then in the awkward situation of seeking another university or higher education post in a centre where she is not 'known'—or indeed she may have to travel from her new home to reach such a centre.

Mobility may of course be a temporary requirement when study abroad is an essential part of qualification. In Portugal in the past, though less so now, postgraduate studies abroad have been customary, especially in scientific subjects where equipment and knowledge of specialised techniques might be unobtainable at home. For women with children, the need to go abroad for such study can present problems: not all husbands, or relations, will be willing to look after the children, even if the mother is ready to accept separation. Hence women may have to postpone such foreign travel at least until the children are older, and this, of course, slows down the woman's academic advancement. Some women in the group interviewed had been in the happy position of being able to study abroad at the same time, in the same place, as their husbands, in some cases embarking on their own course of study mainly because their husband had to study abroad. Others, undertaking such study while younger, had in fact met their future husbands as students in another country.

How do women who teach in Portuguese universities see the 'dual role' of the working mother?

Mobility is affected by marriage and family influences. These factors were obvious in responses to major questions of the enquiry. Women interviewed were asked what they thought were the reasons for the 'pyramid' structure found in analysis of women's positions in teaching in universities in Portugal—i.e. why there were fewer women as the university levels became higher.

Many reasons for this structure were offered: but in 41 cases reference was made to the probable effects of marriage and family on women's careers.

Many of the sample were themselves married, with children, but the comments made were general, indeed on occasion the woman pointed out that she herself had the advantage of a supportive husband, or good arrangements for child care but was referring to the situation of women in general. The marital status of the group was:

Single:	11
Married:	39
Divorced:	6

The numbers of children in the families were:

One child	16
Two children	16
Three children	4
Four children	3
Six children	1

It has to be noted here that 15 of those interviewed were under the age of 35: the single women were in most cases relatively young, hence the marriage rate cannot be regarded as finally determined. Similarly, in some cases the families of the younger women could still be incomplete.

The commonly expressed view was simply that having to look after children imposed great demands on the woman's time and energy, especially while the children were young. Children too, it was pointed out, arrive during the years when the academic worker could be most creative—one woman estimated that she had lost two years of academic advancement in looking after her children— but two women suggested that nowadays there was a tendency for women who took their career seriously to marry late, and have their children after the age of 30, while another commented that to have a child before obtaining the PhD was to make progress in an academic career more difficult. (It was also suggested by three women that there is a growing tendency for women to divorce after they obtain their PhD.) Children's illness inevitably interrupted the woman's work, even if she had people to help her in looking after the child. Another woman gave the opinion—which she said was not now widely accepted—that mothers should be at home with their children at least till the child was two or three years old. Maternity leave, while viewed as a positive recognition of women's rights, could also, two women pointed out, be a handicap both in causing delay in work and in being seen by some employers as an argument against employing a woman. On the practical level, women had normally to go home in the late afternoon to attend to the family's evening meal; this conflicted with university meetings, and sometimes with work in progress—evening meetings in the university could be similarly inconvenient.

At the same time, a number of women were not convinced that children imposed a major handicap. Four suggested that marriage was used as an excuse by women who simply did not want to make the strenuous efforts required by university teaching. Reference was also made to the ready availability of domestic help and child care in Portugal. In the past too, though this was an aspect now changing, the academic woman could count on the assistance of her female relatives to look after children while she was out at work—or even travelling abroad.

In fact domestic help did still seem generally available: the great majority of the group had domestic assistance of some kind, although few now had the 'living in' domestic of earlier decades. The quality of such domestic help admittedly was variable and the suitability of people to look after children has been a problem on a few occasions, but the changes in the employment structure of the country towards greater industrialization and towards a more developed tourist industry did not yet seem to have deprived the working woman in Portugal of this kind of support.

Other factors affecting women at work

If, despite its acknowledged influence, having to look after children did not seem a full explanation for the pyramid structure of women's employment in higher education, what further factors were suggested? In particular, was there lingering prejudice, a denial of women's equality?

There was widespread agreement (36 women pointed it out) that women have—legally—equal opportunities in Portugal. Two or three women suggested that indeed, traditionally, Portuguese society has been a matriarchy in which women played the dominating role in the family. Many recalled the dominating character-istics of their own mother or grandmother and said that within their own families there had certainly not been any discrimination against females. But it was also pointed out that in the life of society outside the university women, in practice, are not treated equally. Men find it easier to gain employment and to be promoted: women are particularly vulnerable in a labour crisis. In the legal profession there is reluctance to accept women as judges or magistrates and in the civil service, the same tendency to appoint women only to the lower levels is evident. Women have difficulties in advancing in politics. Less able men, commented one woman, particularly resent competition from women. Lower class husbands were said to be less tolerant of a wife's work outside the home. Drunkenness and associated violence against women were said to be still present in the lives of the working class.

Class differences, and the greater disadvantages for women in rural areas, were mentioned by ten respondents. It is still difficult for girls of lower social class to gain higher education whereas even before the Revolution, it was asserted, middle class girls had a fair chance of education, including higher education.

A 'neutral' explanation was offered by three women who thought that the minority situation of women at the top levels in universities derives from the years when women less frequently attended university, and, consequently, men were appointed to the top positions which they now hold. Earlier, too, more men would have taken higher qualifications. It seemed therefore to be a question simply of time before more women reached the higher levels. But one woman discounted this argument, saying that by now enough time had elapsed for the natural increase in women's numbers at higher levels to have taken place, if nothing else stood in the way.

Another 'neutral' explanation was the great attraction of secondary school teaching for women graduates. This career, according to 13 women, seems to many girls to offer a socially acceptable occupation and the chance to combine work easily with home duties. It avoids the stresses of study for higher qualifications and appointments. (For many years it could be entered without professional training (de Almeida, 1981).) In fact, 24 of the group had intended to teach in secondary school or had done so for some years. At the same time it should be mentioned that six women had very firmly decided on no account to teach, mainly because of the unpleasant conditions of classroom life, 'noisy brats', poor discipline—though those who had opted to teach had frequently been influenced by the wish to imitate their admired teachers. (Here one has to bear in mind the changes in the school system, the differences between city and rural schools, and the growth of coeducational and comprehensive schools in post-revolutionary times.)

Opinions were divided as to whether prejudice against women had been eliminated from universities. Some women perceived the university as free from past prejudices—though one commented that in the past men had regarded women as attractive additions to the department (though of course in lower-ranking positions). Other women, more often themselves at senior levels, said that there are still macho views and that while all may be well at the lower levels, prejudice, though veiled, remains at the top. Four women claimed that for advancement women have to do more than men. In two cases women were convinced that they had not been received at the agregação because they were women, though such prejudice is of course difficult to prove. (One commented bitterly that, according to the comments male members of the jury made to her afterwards, so many of them had voted for her to succeed that she really must have received a majority of positive votes.) Professors, though legally bound to help junior colleagues to advance in their career (and some women had benefited by such help), could stop advancement simply by inaction and did so, on occasion. One woman noted that in an important case she and a female colleague had simply not been told about a vacancy. There remains still the view that men are the breadwinners. There are covert, unspoken pressures on women. It was also pointed out that some institutions of higher education and some faculties remain male-dominated, especially the technological universities, with large majorities of male students. Thus, while women may be found as students and teachers in science faculties of universities, male dominance is still solidly entrenched in the applied sciences.

The point was also made, on occasion, that prejudice may not be sexist: it may also operate against those suspected of the 'wrong' political views; or in a narrower academic field, it may operate against those who do not seem to have studied the right specialisms, e.g. in medicine or some physical sciences.

Women's own attitudes were also mentioned as possible reasons for lack of advancement. Women, individuals suggested, were not interested in getting to the top: they disliked bureaucracy. Women are unwilling to fight for positions, and they may lack confidence in their own abilities, while men are positively urged on—women should be more ready to compete, they should have more self-confidence. Women may prefer family life to an academic career. But one woman commented that women are tough and tenacious, whereas men are more speculative.

Comparisons with Other Findings

On major issues the results from this survey in Portugal reinforce information gained by surveys in other countries. Given the same pyramid structure of women's teaching careers in universities, women in Portugal note the very great effect of women's other role in bearing and caring for children. What is interesting is that the difference in the availability of domestic or family help does not seem materially to reduce the influence of family concerns. Here one can recall that in the countries studied earlier (Sutherland, 1985a), the greater provision of kindergarten and creche places in East Germany did not seem to resolve the situation of the working mother—though in that society, there were perhaps greater practical difficulties of shopping and domestic work. But again, the better provisions in France and Finland for child care similarly did not seem the whole answer to the problem.

A further point of similarity, not so far discussed, is sex bias in choice of subjects. Such bias has been widely found (Moore, 1987). In some respects Portugal shows an unusual distribution of women students for although there is the customary predominance of females in the humanities, there are greater proportions of women in science faculties and even in applied sciences. In 1986–87, women students were 79.8% of those studying for degrees in Arts (with teacher preparation), 66.9% in Physical and Biological Sciences (with teacher preparation), 59.7% in Medical Sciences, 25.2% in Engineering Sciences (CEPES, 1988). Here one must again note the association of studies with preparation for school teaching. (Something of this trend, though less marked, was evident in West Germany; and in the United Kingdom, the tendency of women graduates to opt more often than men to enter school teaching is well known.) Thus women's more frequent entry into scientific studies in Portugal (or in other countries) does not necessarily greatly change their future employment prospects. Similarly, while women are found in greater numbers in engineering studies in Portugal than in many other educational systems, they again tend to cluster in certain areas—chemical engineering, notably, is their major interest. Whether increasing enrolment in engineering studies will develop is uncertain—much may depend on consequent employment opportunities and, as we have seen, there remain prejudices in favour of men in industry. Nevertheless, such variations in sex differences in choices of study remain worthy of further attention: they affect not only women's employment prospects in general but also their possibilities to rise in higher education, possibilities which are reduced if women cluster in too few areas.

As we have noted, the formal procedures for appointment do seem to give women equal chances to progress in academic careers in Portugal and women themselves are clearly aware of the qualifications needed. Two points of possible difficulty remain—mobility when study abroad is required (which women may adjust to by various means) or when a change of residence has to be made for family reasons, and the prejudices which may be concealed in some assessing and interviewing procedures even in an apparently 'open' system. In other countries also, mobility is certainly a common problem; so are some actions of committees which can allow hidden prejudices against women to take effect. Therefore one must welcome the growing tendency (instanced in the Commission of the European Communities proposals for positive action in reviewing policies of appointment and interviewing, and in Australian Affirmative Action policies) to look critically at the practical processes by which appointments and promotions are made and to study the resulting staff structures.

But it remains to be seen whether such action will be efficacious. In Portugal there is the belief that universities are less prejudiced than society in general. Such a belief is common in Europe: in societies generally, industry seems the sector where prejudice dies hard, though other professions are not without indications of disadvantage to qualified women. Within universities in Portugal and elsewhere, opinions differ as to the absence of prejudice (among male students as well as among male staff): some women claim to be unaware of such prejudice, others are convinced of its influence. Proof of the intervention of prejudices is remarkably hard to establish but it could be a factor frustrating the optimistic career expectations of the younger generation of women who are now numerous at the lower levels of the career in Portugal.

Another factor which could frustrate such optimistic expectations is governmental policy in funding university posts: it is still not clear whether the end of the expansionist stage in Portuguese higher education will soon limit promotion possibilities as has been happening in some European systems—though others, e.g. France, currently experience increases.

But so far as women's employment in higher education is concerned, one has to remember not only the 'pecking order' among institutions (with women being employed in the less prestigious), one has also to take into account changes in the pecking order of professions, and especially changes in the status of the profession of university teaching. In various European countries one hears it said that this status is becoming lower. (In Portugal, there is the curious provision that university teachers formally declaring that they do not have other paid posts, receive a large bonus.) If men see more attractive outlets in other professions, where pay, promotion prospects, prestige are better, women may find university posts easier to obtain (though they too might begin to opt for better paid and more prestigious work). Thus the future developments of university or other higher education teaching as a career for women remain unpredictable, but the similarities in women's situation in higher education in so many European countries do seem evidence of wide general influences and common traditions. Change may therefore be a matter not of reforms within individual educational systems but of response to wider international trends.

References

AAA (Affirmative Action Agency) (1987) *Affirmative Action: Guidelines for Implementation in Institutions of Higher Education*. Canberra: Australian Government Publishing Service.

Braga, C. Lloyd and Grilo, E. Marçal (1981) Ensino Superior. In M. Silva and M. Isabel Tamen (eds) *Sistema de Ensino em Portugal* (pp 223–57). Lisboa: Fundação Calouste Gulbenkian.

CEPES (Centre Européen Pour l'Enseignement Supérieur) (1988) *Proceedings of Symposium on the Role of Women in Higher Education, in Research and in the Planning and Administration of Education*. Bucharest: CEPES.

Commission of the European Communities (1988) Positive action – equal opportunities for women in employment. *Social Europe* 1/89, 66–8.

de Almeida, E. P. (1981) Formação de Professores. In M. Silva and M. Isabel Tamen (eds) *Sistema de Ensino em Portugal* (pp 413–44). Lisboa: Fundacão Calouste Gulbenkian.

Heseltine, E. (1987) *Alice in Academe*. Stockholm: Swedish National Board of Universities and Colleges.

IEA (International Association for the Evaluation of Educational Achievement) (1988) *Science Achievement in Seventeen Countries*. Oxford: Pergamon Press.

Moore, K. M. (1987) Women's access and opportunity in higher education: Toward the twenty-first century. *Comparative Education* 23, 1, 23–34.

Ruivo, B. (1985) Représentation des femmes dans l'enseignement supérieur et la recherche scientifique. Lisbon: UNESCO (conference paper).

Schriewer, J. and Holmes, B. (eds) (1988) *Theories and Methods in Comparative Education*. Frankfurt am Main, New York: Peter Lang Verlag.

Sutherland, M.B. (1985a) The situation of women who teach in universities: Contrasts and common ground. *Comparative Education* 21, 1, 21–8.

—— (1985b) *Women Who Teach in Universities*. Stoke on Trent: Trentham Books for the European Institute of Education and Social Policy.

UNESCO (1982) *Study on the Portrayal of Women and Men in School Textbooks and Children's Literature in the Ukrainian Soviet Republic*. Paris: UNESCO.

—— (1983) *A Study of the Portrayal of Women and Men in School Textbooks and Children's Literature in France*. Paris: UNESCO.

—— (1987) *Enquête sur la représentation des femmes dans l'enseignement supérieur, la recherche, la planification et la gestion de l'éducation: réalisée avec le concours de la Féderation Internationale des Femmes Diplômées des Universités*. Paris: UNESCO.

RESEARCH REPORTS

Women Engineers: Conditions at University and in the Profession

Directors: Professor Dr Hedwig Rudolph
Dr Doris Janshen
Technical University of Berlin

Funding: Grants from Federal West German Ministry of Education and
Science and the Technical University of Berlin

Timespan: 1984–1986

The project studied 90 women and 20 men in mechanical and electrical engineering, three out of five enrolled as students at two universities, one in Berlin and one in Aachen; the rest were professional engineers in the respective regions. The study, conducted over the period 1984–1986, was not, however, a traditional empirical study based on structured samples aimed at generalisation or replication. It set out to be a *qualitative, diagnostic* study based on depth and complexity of interaction of factors, rather than breadth and brevity in order to cover larger numbers.

The complex and lengthy interviews (often from 6–8 hours) set out to investigate the specific social conditions and personal characteristics which appear to have made it possible for some women to succeed in a male-dominated profession *despite their isolation.* The project was policy-oriented, and the very detailed transcripts (over 10,000 pages) and taxonomies of relevant influential factors, have resulted in the development of a 'catalogue of measures' to ease women's integration into the engineering profession *without the price of over-adaptation to male patterns of behaviour.*

The project's analyses suggest that most of the female students looked back on their schools as a negative environment in terms of encouragement for their own personality development. This was despite a mainly positive retrospective memory of maths/science learning as such, achieved for over half of the women by early specialisation. But they entered higher education with 'a postponed search for identity and a reservoir of conflicts to match'. The study supports the view that those women who survive into and through university engineering schools, tend to be relatively more gifted than their male peers, and that *average* female pupils are much less likely than average male pupils to be encouraged to take up engineering. The gifted who did survive, were seen to need strategies to survive in what is described as 'the harsh climate' of a confrontationist engineering world in which male students did not feel secure in recognising female academic competence.

The study concludes, *inter alia,* that generalised and national strategies are not useful, but that institutionally-based programmes which reflect local conditions are needed. The researchers argue in particular for a better *mentor* system.

Address for correspondence: Professor Dr Hedwig Rudolph, Director, Institut fur Sozial-Wissenschaften in Erziehung und Ausbildung, Fachbereich 22, Technical University of Berlin, Franklinstrasse 28/29, D1000 Berlin 10, Federal Republic of Germany.

Women in Science & Technology in Australia: Policy Review Project (UQ WISTA)

Director: Professor Eileen Byrne
                       Department of Education
                       University of Queensland

Funding: Australian Research Grants Scheme
                       Australian Research Council
                       The University of Queensland
                       The Myer Foundation
                       The Commonwealth Tertiary Education Commission

Timespan: 1985–1989

The University of Queensland WISTA Policy Review project (UQ WISTA) re-examines factors which hinder or help women's access to and progression in science and technology, using a mainly qualitative research methodology. Its theoretical framework uses Glaser & Strauss's approach to grounded theory as a central method. The project set out to review ten factors of potential influence, viz. same-sex role models; mentors; image of science and technology; male and female peer attitudes; single-sex schooling vs. coeducation; prerequisites and curricular choice; maths as a critical filter; careers education and vocational guidance; women's support networks; affirmative action intervention strategies. These factors have been re-examined against four dimensions: institutional ecology, critical mass theory, male and female attribution of disciplines, and structure and style of disciplines.

The project has examined twenty or so scientific and technological disciplines using five major Universities and five Institutes of Technology as a source for data to support or challenge current theory and received wisdom, and to help the development of new grounded theory and of mid-range theory in a policy context.

Conclusions so far challenge several areas of current assumptive knowledge. Firstly, it is argued that research focus and policy approaches should be realigned to concentrate on the influence of institutional ecology, institutional culture and systemic factors rather than examining the behaviour of girls and women: that is moving from the blaming-the-victim approach to examining the failure of those who set up and control learning environments. Elements in institutional ecology include, *inter alia*, the male/female balance (above or below critical mass thresholds); discourse styles; structure, content and learning environment of different disciplines; and role modelling and mentorship. In the case of the latter, while the data do not contradict the well-supported theory that same-sex-role models help to break the sex-role stereotype, there appears to be no empirical evidence whatever to support the widely-held hypothesis that active same-sex-role modelling by women in higher education is at all correlated with actual increases in female enrolments or with changes in female behaviour in curricular choice or vocational aspiration or expectation. Conversely, UQ WISTA data and analyses suggest that mentorship is highly influential, but continues to be widely underestimated. Data from the UQ WISTA project also supports current critical mass theory. A correlation between the image, structure and location of disciplines on the one hand and high or low female recruitment and progression on the other, appears consistent and widespread. New grounded theory on the influence of institutional ecology is also being developed.

The UQ WISTA project supports the need to revise research methodological practice to move from *dyadic* (two-factor) approaches to examining *related clusters* of factors; and a shift to examining separate and particular disciplines and subdisciplines in greater depth, rather than attempting to study 'science' or 'technology' as areas of study.

A new follow-through project (the SHEP-APIST project) begins in 1990 to look further at the remaining clusters of factors (prerequisites, curricular choice, careers education, vocational guidance, image) in the upper years of secondary schooling.

Note

The UQ WISTA project is one of three Australian WISTA projects nearing completion. The other two are based at the University of New South Wales, School of Microbiology under the direction of Dr Elizabeth Hazel, who initiated the original three-stranded WISTA project.

Correspondence: Interim research reports on the findings so far are available for relevant researchers in the field from Professor Eileen Byrne, Director, UQ WISTA Project, Department of Education, University of Queensland, ST LUCIA QLD 4067.

BOOK REVIEWS

In a Different Voice: Psychological Theory and Women's Development
Carol Gilligan, Cambridge, Mass: Harvard University Press, 1982, Pp. 184. ISBN
0-674-44543-0 (cloth). ISBN 0-674-44544-9 (paper).

In 1988 Carol Gilligan edited *Mapping the Moral Domain: A Contribution of Women's Thinking to Psychological Theory and Education*. It is an appropriate time to look again at her important 1982 work, *In a Different Voice*, which exposed the theoretical failure of psychological theories of development to come to terms with women's experience, a failure very relevant to those concerned with women's and men's learning experiences, and with gender-bias and gender-neutrality in the schooling process.

Hierarchy and web are the two visual images that Carol Gilligan uses in *In a Different Voice* to suggest different, gender-related approaches to relationships that determine quite different ways in which moral development can be traced. These two visual images—the hierarchy or ladder representing a linear order of inequality, a rigid frame of steps, and the web representing a multi-directional order of equality on a flexible frame—pervade the book. Yet an auditory image evoked in the title, the voice, best expresses the impact of the book. The book is a sounding of voices, their interplay, their harmony and cacophany. And Gilligan's voice itself is so articulate and eloquent in her analysis of the language of others that the best review of the book might be an echo.

Throughout her discussion, Gilligan presents the voices of women and men, boys and girls, as they discuss both hypothetical and real moral dilemmas and how they deal with them. Her representation of two modes of interpreting the relationship between other and self is based on years of experience in research and teaching, 'listening to people talking about morality and themselves' and recognising that 'women's *voices sounded distinct*' (p.1). She includes the voices not only of theorists and those whom she interviewed in her studies but also of an array of literary characters—for example, Maggie Tulliver in *Mill on the Floss* deciding whether to renounce the man she loves out of loyalty to her cousin to whom he is engaged and Margaret Drabble's Jane Grey in *The Waterfall*, having a similar dilemma but making a different decision.

Part of a contemporary questioning of the claims that science and language are neutral, Gilligan's book shows how women have been excluded in the building of psychological theories having implications for moral development. She identifies what has been seen as a problem in women's development—women's moral 'immaturity' compared with men—as a failure to base representations of human development on women's as well as men's experience.

Gilligan uses as a basis for her discussion material obtained from three studies, all depending on interviews that include questions focused on self-concept, morality, and choices in difficult situations. Gilligan's research method differs from that used in many studies of moral judgment in that she does not limit interviewees to a responsive role in thinking about hypothetical problems presented to them but also asks people to describe what they perceive as moral problems and conflicts in their own lives. One study was of twenty-five students in Bachelor's degree study, randomly selected from a group who had decided in their second year of study to take one course in moral and political choice. Another study involved a sample of 144 persons, eight males and eight females at each of nine points across the life cycle from ages 6–9, to 60, matched for age, intelligence, education, occupation, and social class. Still another study involved exploring the experiences and thoughts of 29 women making a decision about whether to have an abortion. The reason for Gilligan's attention to women's abortion decisions is that she considers this to be a domain in which the conflict between self and other is most clearly embodied and in which 'women have the power to choose and thus are willing to speak in their own voice' (pp.69–70). This aspect of the study is a necessary corrective to studies in which the unique concerns of males are taken as universal and women's concerns are seen as deviant. Here women's concerns and their thinking about moral decisions are central.

In her critique of psychological theories, Gilligan begins with Freud, who saw women's continuing pre-Oedipal attachments to their mothers and their lack of castration anxiety as impediments to the development of the superego. In a brief discussion of major voices in psychological literature such as Kohlberg, Piaget, and Erikson, she interrogates the claim of Freud and his successors, referring to Nancy Chodorow, for example, who sees girls' close identity with their mothers as a strength, allowing them to have an inclusive definition of the self and to see themselves as more closely related to the external world.

Much of the power of *In a Different Voice* derives from excerpts from the transcripts of interviews and her analysis of what her interviewees say. For example, when Gilligan shows how matched sixth grade children, Jake and Amy, respond to the Kohlberg hypothetical moral dilemma, in which a man named Heinz cannot afford a drug that will save his dying wife, she calls into question the adequacy of accepted theories to describe the girl's process of resolving a moral problem. In response to the question, 'Should Heinz steal the drug?' Jake replies with confidence that he should, because life is more important than property. However, Amy's responses seem initially naive and confused. It becomes clear, however, as Gilligan follows Amy's thinking that Amy interprets the question not as '*Should* Heinz steal the drug?' but as 'should Heinz *steal* the drug?' The moral problem for her is not that of whether the life of Heinz's wife is more important than the druggist's property but whether the druggist should respond to the woman's need, precluding any need for stealing. Amy sees the problem in a larger context of relationships within a community over a period of time. She sees that stealing would result in Heinz's imprisonment, which would harm not only Heinz but also his wife, who would necessarily be abandoned. The girl's response shows a moral sophistication that would not be recognised by traditional theorists.

Further discussions of self concept and morality with Jake and Amy provide the basis for Gilligan's elucidation of another major difference that she associates with gender. Responsibility as perceived by the boy requires that he limit his action and restrain aggression in order to avoid interference with others. Responsibility as perceived by the girl requires action on behalf of others. For the boy harm is seen to grow out of aggression; for the girl harm is seen to grow out of a failure to respond, indifference and lack of concern. 'To Jake, responsibility means *not doing* what he wants because he is thinking of others; to Amy, it means *doing* what others are counting on her to do regardless of what she herself wants' (p.38).

These interviews with children not only dramatically expose the inadequacy of research on children's moral development but also challenge educators of girls and boys, especially moral educators in schools.

One of the most intriguing features of *In a Different Voice* and one very relevant to the learning process is its presentation of the results of an analysis of male and female responses to the Thematic Apperception Test (TAT), requiring that respondents invent stories based on pictures. In a 1982 study conducted by Gilligan and Susan Pollak, Pollak observed that men's stories based on what appeared to be peaceful scenes often contained violent imagery, whereas women projected no violence into the same scenes. Gilligan and Pollak hypothesised that men and women 'construe danger in different ways' (p.40). Although other studies to which Gilligan refers showed generally a greater violence in stories by men, Gilligan and Pollak found sex differences not only in frequency of violent imagery but also in the kinds of stimuli that evoked violent imagery. When pictures represented people in closer proximity, men's use of violent imagery in stories related to the pictures increased. On the other hand, when pictures represented people alone or far apart, the violence in the women's stories was intensified. '*The women in the class projected violence most frequently into the picture of the man at his desk (the only picture portraying a person alone), while the men in the class most often saw violence in the scene of the acrobats on the trapeze (the only picture in which people touched). Thus it appears that men and women experience attachment and separation in different ways and that each sex perceives a danger which the other does not—men in connection, women in separation*' (p. 42). Gilligan points out that women often imagined that, in the situation depicting a man and woman on a trapeze, a safety net was in place. Women, by elaborating on the picture, protected the lives of their characters. Men interpreting women's invention of the net have seen the absence of violence in such a story as a repression of aggressive impulses. However, Gilligan suggests that women '. . . *try to change the rules in order to preserve relationships; men in abiding by rules depict relationships as easily replaced*' (p.44). Gilligan's explication raises broad educational questions concerning the way women and men perceive, conceptualise, and compensate for insufficient information.

The basis for understanding women's and men's moral development is what Gilligan calls 'the paradoxical truths of human experience—that we know ourselves as separate only insofar as we live in connection with others, and that we experience relationship only insofar as we differentiate other from self' (p.63). If masculinity is defined through separation and femininity is defined through attachment, then both men and women, Gilligan suggests, have equivalent but opposite developmental problems. Men develop fully if they not only see themselves as separate but also come to terms with intimacy. Women develop fully if they not only see themselves in relation to others but can also come to terms with individuation.

Gilligan refers to Kohlberg's use of Piaget in distinguishing three perspectives on moral conflict—preconventional (focused on the needs of the self), conventional (based on shared norms of communities), and postconventional (reflecting the construction of moral principles that are universal in application). She sees women's discussions of the abortion decision as revealing these three perspectives. The first perspective is reflected in women's attachment of highest priority to survival, against the world; the second is reflected in a shift toward social partici- pation and conventional ideas of goodness and unselfishness which, however, define the self in relation only to the self's value to other people; the third entails inclusion of the self as a person needing care and concern along with others and attention to the intentions and consequences of the abortion rather than the opinions of others. Gilligan claims that at this stage care becomes a universal injunction to care for both the self and the other, representing the highest form of postconventional morality for women. She observes, too, that postconventional morality may display itself in women as a renunciation of moral judgment in a situation in which injustice and suffering are inevitable in the very construction of the dilemma, whether hypothetical or real (pp.100–101).

The book sharply focuses on individuals talking about themselves as individuals, with little reference to the social or cultural context and influential factors related to but distinct from gender. Although Gilligan is careful to state that she is not theorising about gender but is using differences associated empirically with gender to distinguish two modes of thought, the relentless consistency of the empirical association tends to subvert that cautionary note, especially in the absence of attempts to suggest alternative theories or variations of the psychoanalytical theories whose inadequacies she demonstrates. But her book is generative, presenting hypotheses to be tested, extended and considered in relation to other analyses to which she refers, such as Jean Baker Miller's work on relationships of dominance and subordination. The book seems to reflect a scholarly decision that parallels the women's moral decisions that Gilligan describes : an emphasis on the richness of concrete or real situations rather than rules governing all situations. Its highly personal stories of moral conflict and their compelling analysis have had and will continue to have influence in such fields as education, women's studies, philosophy, religion, ethics, literary studies, social work, and psychology. The book has crucial implications for educators who face questions of how best to facilitate learning for people—men and women—who vary widely in the way they view themselves and the world.

Linda Conrad
Griffith University

Analyzing Gender: A Handbook of Social Science Research
Beth B. Hess and Myra Marx Ferree (eds). Newbury Park, Ca: Sage Publications, 1987. Pp. 580. ISBN 0-8039-2719-3.

After two decades of detailed research on sex differences, gender construction and the status, position and experiences of women and girls, the appearance of a tightly-edited, scholarly and contemporary synthesis of current social science research on issues involving gender is greatly to be welcomed. Hess and Ferree have achieved a notable and significant consolidation of the state of our current knowledge and understanding about gender in society, albeit from primarily women's perspectives. This excellent collection of contributions moves us from what the editors describe as the '*add-women-and-stir*' formula, to a range of research perspectives which (correctly) involve the *incorporation* of women and gender into the basic paradigms of research.

It has to be said that the volume title is misleading. The review unavoidably covers work on women considerably more than work on gender, since gender research so far has rightly focused on the area of most disadvantage. But its subtitle of *A Handbook of Social Science Research* does not reflect the actual editorial limitation to 'an overview of feminist perspectives in the social sciences today' (p.10). There is significant research which breaks new ground on gender (including work on the education of girls) which is *not* feminist, but which is none the less seminal, is new and has shifted paradigms.

The selection of issues to be covered is not wholly well balanced. Five chapters on aspects of the sexuality issues, and five on work, development and economic contexts may seem excessive in a research review which contains no treatment at all of the major new research thrusts in reviewing gender in education, in vocational training, in learning and teaching environments and in education's role in *controlling* precisely those arenas of work, economic activity and social policy which have locked women into domestic, internal, dependent and less qualified sections of those arenas. It has been above all the schools—including preschools— and the men who control education systems who have so strongly contributed to the kinds of cultural construction of artificially exclusive sex roles, to the detriment of girls and women, which this volume reviews.

There are, notwithstanding, many scholarly and innovative chapters here which educators are strongly recommended to read. For educators themselves suffer from precisely the same parochialism of over-specialised discipline bases, which has caused the exclusion of education as such from a women's studies review. The reasons why boys and girls, male and female teachers may behave as they do, lie partially in the kind of issues raised by this volume.

Janet Sayers discusses a reconceptualisation of science in a feminist critique. Her treatment spans several dimensions, from a criticism of the misuse of a debased form of science to underpin theories of sex differentiation and alleged female inferiority, to what she describes as 'the recent rejection of science by feminism'. This is an oddly elliptic concept; it is not surely science as such, but its artificial construction, structure, content and image on a male-dominated paradigm which has been up for review. Sayers' treatment is a good, if selective review. She records how the historical founding of social relations on religious orthodoxy has shifted to scientifically-supported social relations based on what Jordanova described as 'a secular, empirically based knowledge of the natural and social world'. But this carried with it ricochets from evolutionary theory, endocrinology and neurological research which, in the lack of scientific objectivity which Sayers exposes, wrongly accredited forms of biological determinism which have led to the constant misinterpretation of data to women's disadvantage. Sayers' review of women's exclusion from science, and their rejection of some forms of science, is set in a holistic conceptual resetting which is valuable reading for science educators—and for any who anachronistically judge the children in their classrooms against theories of biological determinism.

Education has been influenced by the Church, by Ministers, by religion and by socially constructed and accredited forms of morality, from the earliest days of schooling. Sheila Briggs' review of women and religion is a relevant reconceptualisation of religion as a major cultural reinforcement of modern industrial patriarchy into a force for innovation and change which accredits a feminisation of ministry. The move of the Church from controlling all main areas of social life and public policy (including education and schooling up to the mid 19th century), to a focus on marriage, family and morality, provides the springboard of her review of two mainstream issues: equal access to all of the Church's roles (the ordination issue) and the recognition of a distinctive women's voice and discourse (the inclusive language and communication issues). Her discussion of the dilemma of the simultaneous need to be identified with male colleagues as equal and the same, and yet to recognise the need to give a 'feminine face to the pastoral care' (p.413), has transferable overtones to our dilemmas about women's generally different styles of educational management and perceived more pastoral role in teaching. And her treatment of the implications of feminist theology and ethics, and of research 'that makes the religious history of women integral to women's history as a whole' (p.423), is important reading for those who control and lead Church schooling (including the Sisterhoods to whose work in founding and developing schools and colleges she pays tribute).

The holistic approach is also evident in Evelyn Nakano Glenn's discussion of 'Gender and the Family', of equal relevance to teachers and to education administrators in these days of the divided and reconstructed families from which our schoolchildren come. She looks at developments against three questions. How have social scientists thought about the family? What further challenges does feminist reconstruction of family, face? These are reviewed through examining the traditional applications of structural functionalism, exchange theory and interactionism, which have perpetuated a monolithic model of the family. Feminist theorists have challenged this monolithic view by looking at the family's constituent elements: the ideology of motherhood (which lets fatherhood off the hook of responsibility); the hierarchy of power within the family, including child abuse, battered wives, economic dependency; resources in the family. But the family is also 'an alternative value system and the main institution for socialising children to resist dominant group culture and authority' (p.373). Glenn's analysis is a valuable source of new thinking for those concerned with the school/family interface, although unlike most other contributors, she fails to draw an overall conclusion of the implications of her review. The editorial stance that the volume aimed to move from *questions* (challenges to standard paradigms) to *answers* (p.10), is not wholly met here.

Space does not permit a detailed review of all of the chapters. Those interested in the school:work:employment interface will find Myra Ferree's review of gender and class, and of conforming and nonconforming behaviour, a useful updating. It highlights in particular, the need to move further away from the concept of 'nontraditionality' and towards 'a more integrated picture of paid work and family responsibilities for both (sexes)' (p.339). This is a theme further developed in Christine Bose's chapter on 'Dual Spheres', which concludes that 'the dual spheres concept has supported patriarchy (but) similar separate-but-equal spheres arguments have supported racism. The two ideologies together helped delimit white male competition for high paying jobs' (p.282). Other relevant chapters deal with such issues as evolutionary perspectives on gender hierarchy, (Christine Ward Gailey), popular culture and the portrayal of women (Muriel Cantor), and gender and political life (Martha Ackelsberg and Irene Diamond). Notwithstanding my reservations expressed earlier, this is an outstanding collection overall and a valuable consolidation of the current state-of-the-art in gender research.

Eileen Byrne
University of Queensland

A Gender Agenda
Terry Evans. Sydney: Allen & Unwin, 1988. Pp. 163. ISBN 0-04-303009-2.

The ample evidence of the social and economic disadvantages faced by Australian women has long prompted inquiry into gender aspects of schooling in Australia, of which the two Commonwealth Schools Commission Reports: *Girls, School & Society* (1975) and *Girls and Tomorrow* (1984) particularly highlight the need to look at the formative years. There is still a need however, for empirical data which analyses the nature of schools, and particularly, the ways in which schooling perpetuates and even induces sex stereotypic attitudes and behaviour. Evans' book, subtitled *A Sociological Study of Teachers, Parents and Pupils in their Primary Schools*, and the result of a research project undertaken from September 1983 to February 1985, might be expected to provide such data.

The project aims as stated by the author were 'to demonstrate the links between the social structural features of society, especially gender, and the social processes which surround and comprise schools'. The notion that schools and society operate in tandem is a sound one; schools are not isolated laboratories of human endeavour, and no study of schooling can be complete without a recognition of the complex web involving parents, government and community. Evans' differentiation of three *gender agendas* at the levels of the *personal* school member, the *collective* school agenda and a broader *societal* agenda is useful. Having said this, and whilst applauding the author's efforts to integrate the different levels, one is forced to look carefully for new light being thrown on the links and the processes.

The research by Evans and his assistant concentrated on two primary schools in Victoria's Latrobe district: Tordale, a 4-teacher, 75-pupil school in a rural community, and Linfield, a town school with 25 teachers and 450 pupils. He employs a variety of methods to collect data, ranging from analysis of local census figures, study of school documents, and observation of meetings and classes, through to interviews of teachers, parents and pupils.

This brings me to the first and most serious weakness of the study: the limited sample chosen. Although the author claims the schools are broadly representative of Australian schools, they are still only two with a *total* teacher cohort of only 29. Given, moreover, the highly urbanised and multi-ethnic nature of the Australian population, it is questionable whether the sample can be seen as 'broadly representative' in sociological terms.

Evans and his co-researcher spent a good deal of time observing and recording meetings and interviewing people. These efforts produced some valuable insight into the workings of school councils, possibly the most valuable section of the book. We witness, for example, the manouvrings of the school principal to get the 'right people' on council, and the way in which apathy on the part of parents enables teachers to control the council agenda. Evans provides us with two case studies of councils at work, contrasting the way in which one council pushes through debate about buying a ride-on mower for the school, achieving a 'victory', whilst another council, lobbied by a mothers' group to bring in changes to the health and human relationships curriculum, fails. The writer's interpretation of these case studies, however, is dubious in its over-simplistic level of explanation, implying as he does that the reason the father in the first scenario got through his proposal for the mower was merely because he was male, President of the Council, and able to control the agenda; whilst the second proposal failed because it was pushed by women and effectively blocked by a male Principal. The issues

are not comparable. The acquisition of a mower is a simple matter of financial priority for a defined purpose. The latter, by contrast, is fraught with controversy, with its issues of morality, sexuality, curriculum control and teacher autonomy in complex interplay. To blame the failure of the mothers' group to bring about change (against the wishes of staff) on the operation of a sexist agenda, is highly suspect in oversimplicity.

Notwithstanding these criticisms, there is some valuable insight to be teased out of this book. For example, after broad discussion of the sex ratio and power distribution in the Victorian education system, Evans pays close attention to the teachers themselves. Their life backgrounds, attitudes and values are enlightening reading, particularly the section on why they chose teaching, and the difference between male and female teacher commitment and ambitions. There is a very telling comment from one male deputy, who is reported saying: '*The men seem to go for the senior roles (and have) career commitment (and the) women are content to teach in the classroom and do that well. It is unfortunate that women don't go for the responsibility, it is always a problem when mothers see their job as second to the family, which fathers don't.*'

Parents and teachers alike will also find the section on the attitudes of parents and pupils interesting reading, and it would appear that traditional sex roles and expectations are alive and strong in the community. But methodological weaknesses appear here also. Again, because of the very small sample, Evans is forced into making unsatisfying comments such as 'A few of the girls . . .' 'Some of the girls . . .' throughout the section. Rather more serious is a tendency to questionable and quite unsubstantiated generalisation, such as: '*There are now some areas of "men's" work where women's representation is sufficient for them to be an accepted minority, for example, in medicine, dentistry or gardening.*'

What does the study conclude? There is a lengthy discussion of the classroom observation findings. The researchers observed one class from each grade level, with observation lasting one week in each case. One would have wished to see the recording schedule used to monitor teacher–pupil interactions as revealed in Tables 7.1 to 7.9, but no such schedule appears in the book. A real difficulty arises, therefore, when one evaluates the findings on classroom interaction. Firstly, what is meant here by 'interactions'? The author says they recorded only those interactions with a verbal component, not those that were non-verbal, although the latter 'may have been recorded as part of the qualitative record of events' (p. 115). What does this tell us? Are we looking at the results of a systematic checklist, or a somewhat more intuitive methodology used to create 'impressions' of classroom life? If so, we should be told. This is particularly so because of considerable interest in the stated finding that girls initiated more interactions with their teachers than did boys, a finding which runs counter to the main body of current research. Evans also provides an interesting finding when he states that teachers with more egalitarian views were the ones where the girls had the highest teacher-initiated and pupil-initiated scores. This is a promising sign, and has obvious implications for teacher training and in-service education, which are not, however, considered or raised.

Although the author frankly states in the introduction to the book that he intends to skip through a theoretical discussion in order to devote more time to the research findings, one notes some imbalance in and notable omissions from the type of literature to which he does refer. Bourdieu and R.W. Connell are certainly relevant to the study, and deservedly receive central treatment, with

predictable side references to Apple & Giddens. But of much greater relevance is the 1986 work of Judith Whyte, whose seminal book on the GIST study of sex-differentiation in British schools, bears many parallels with this study. Omissions of previous major *research-based* reconceptualisation in the area of interaction in schooling, weaken the basis of the Evans study.

Despite the promises offered early in the book, there is not a great deal of light shed on the links and processes apparently explored. As one reads, one gets the uneasy impression that there is a good deal of 'stretching and filling' taking part in order to reach the desired book length. There is, indeed, value here for parents and teachers, but the research scholar will wish to look at the outcome with a shrewdly critical eye.

Jillian Brannock
Brisbane College of Advanced Education

NOTES ON CONTRIBUTORS

Eileen Byrne is Professor of Education (Policy Studies) at the University of Queensland. As a former Deputy Chief Education Officer in English local government, she is a policymaker turned academic. Author of several books and international reports on the education and training of girls and women, she has recently completed a major four-year research study on women in science and technology, a book on which is to be published in 1990 by Falmer Press Ltd.

Correspondence: Department of Education, The University of Queensland, St Lucia QLD 4067, Australia.

Shirley Sampson is Senior Lecturer in Education at Monash University, Melbourne, and a sociologist by discipline. An experienced researcher in gender issues in education, her recent published work includes a study of gender in teacher promotions, and *Educating Girls: Practice & Research*, co-edited with Gilah Leder (Allen & Unwin, Sydney, 1989).

Correspondence: Dr Shirley Sampson, Faculty of Education, Monash University, Clayton VIC 3168, Australia.

Margaret Sutherland is Emeritus Professor of Education, University of Leeds. She is a Past President of the World Association for Educational Research, Chairman of the Standing Conference on Studies in Education, and holder of the 1986–87 Leverhulme Trust Emeritus Fellowship. Her extensive publications include *Sex Bias in Education* (Blackwell, Oxford, 1981) and her recent international study *Women who Teach in Universities* (Trentham Books, 1985).

Correspondence: 46 The Scores, St Andrews, Fife KY16 9AS, Scotland.

Hildur Ve is Associate Professor in the Institute of Sociology at the University of Bergen, Norway. Her past work includes research on social class differences in young girls' attitudes to education, work and future family. She is currently Director of an innovative action research project aimed at achieving a gender-neutral environment in the first weeks in the early years of schooling.

Correspondence: Institute of Sociology, University of Bergen, N5000 Bergen, Norway.

Linda Conrad is now a lecturer in the Centre for the Advancement of Learning at Griffith University, after some years as the University's Equal Employment Opportunity Coordinator. Before coming to Australia, she directed test development activities at Educational Testing Service in Princeton, NJ, having particular concern for fairness for women and minority groups in standardised tests.

Correspondence: Dr Linda Conrad, Centre for the Advancement of Learning, Griffith University, Nathan QLD 4111, Australia.

Jill Brannock is a Lecturer in the Department of Educational Studies at the Brisbane College of Advanced Education. She is currently conducting research into gender-bias and gender neutrality in Queensland primary and secondary classrooms.

Correspondence: Ms Jill Brannock, Department of Educational Studies, Brisbane College of Advanced Education, Kelvin Grove Campus, Victoria Park Road, Kelvin Grove QLD 4059, Australia.